In God We Trust

A Nation Under Judgment and Call to Repentance

By Carmelita Greco

You can reach Carmelita at TheClarionCall.TV: info@theclarioncall.tv

Cover art by Debbie Clark

ISBN: 979-8-218-12449-6

Table of Contents

Introduction

I wrote this book with a burden on my heart, a burden for America and the people I so deeply care about. I have been so blessed to be born and raised in America, a nation that has historically valued freedom, faith, and hard work. I was born and raised in Southeastern Michigan to very modest beginnings and found that the freedoms our nation has offered were everything I needed to pursue a good life. The freedoms we enjoy and the biblical heritage that brings hope and love for one another were the substance needed for a young girl with many lofty goals. I am saddened that the America I once experienced has progressively slipped away from the foundations it was built upon with a moral fabric that supported family values, belief in God, and servanthood.

We have rebelled against everything that makes our nation worthy of blessing. We rebelled against individual liberty, family values, life, and God Himself. We started by removing prayer from our public schools in the 1960's, followed by removing the ten commandments from our public buildings. As a result, our morality has progressively become more detached and secular. Many of our schools have become war zones and our society has few moral boundaries, the result of which is utter perplexity.

I would like to refer the famed Back to the Future 1 & 2, two 1980's hit films in which a past era representing America in the 1950's was featured. While this era seemed rather peaceful and playful, the future 20th century America, run by criminal figure Biff, was violent, dark, and chaotic. This is the future we are headed toward, and in many cases we have already arrived. Many Americans long for the days of their youth when America was peaceful and safe. This will only be possible again with a restoration of biblical values and a heart of repentance upon the land.

2 Chronicles 7:14 says, "If my people, who are called by my name, will humble themselves and pray and seek my face and turn from their wicked ways, then I will hear from heaven, and I will forgive their sin and will heal their land." (NIV)

During his sermon in 1630, our pilgrim founder, John Winthrop, quotes Matthew 5:14 and dreams of a city on a hill, a beacon of hope for the nations, if we follow the call of God. This noble intent has been partially realized, but in recent years we have seen a deep moral decline, a war on our freedoms and a rise in political corruption.

The blessing of God comes with a devoted alignment with the Word of God and the ways of God. When we neglect the call for righteousness, we set ourselves up for judgment in the same way nations were judged in the past.

Many people have replaced the God of our foundation with gods of gold and silver (the bull market) and false and foreign gods, resulting in a lack of morality, a war on life, increased crime, division, and utter bewilderment.

People are more confused today than they have ever been. Moral absolutes and truth are no longer taught as constants in our public institutions and schools. Science has been replaced with philosophies that fit new moral ideology, shifting gender, marriage, and justice. These shifts in culture have brought forward a morality that allows a woman to eliminate a child even after birth without criminal penalty, California Bill AB 2223. In addition, children are taught to choose a gender over accepting the birth gender that God gave them. Divorce and promiscuous sexual activity are also on the rise, along with an increase in sexually transmitted diseases. Also, frequent gun violence in our schools, human trafficking, lawlessness, and suicide are steadily increasing. The national moral shift has flipped the moral compass upside down and left our society in ruins. Isaiah 5:20 says, "Woe unto them that call evil good, and good evil; that put darkness for light, and light for darkness; that put bitter for sweet, and sweet for bitter!" (KJV)

I felt a personal burden by the Lord to release this message. God is faithful in telling His people what is coming before it happens to prepare our hearts and to strengthen our faith. This book reveals a message of sure judgment coming upon the nation and the restoration of a remnant of God's people in America.

There have been deep seeds sown into the soil of this nation, and in these final days before the return of Christ, the seeds that have been planted will blossom. A restoration of God's Spirit will revive the spiritually lukewarm church and bring many people to encounter Jesus in this season of testing and judgment. It is time to brace ourselves for tribulation. Wars and rumors of wars are at our door, along with inflation, increased global insecurity, and potential food shortages. Jesus said in John 16:33, "I have told you all this so that you may have peace in me. Here on earth, you will have many trials and sorrows. But take heart, because I have overcome the world." (NLT)

The hope for our nation is found in our biblical inheritance and the person of Jesus Christ. He is our eternal hope that we can set our hearts on. He is our salvation and the foundation we can stand upon. We must return to "In God We Trust."

Chapter 1
A Messenger and a Message

I am just a messenger delivering a message. I don't hold myself in high esteem. If we seek the Lord with all our hearts and posture them toward His will, He will reveal His thoughts. Numbers 22:28 declares that God even spoke through a donkey: "Then the Lord opened the donkey's mouth, and it said to Balaam, 'What have I done to you to make you beat me these three times?'" (NIV)

I love the humor of the Lord. He uses the weak things of this world to confound the wise. He doesn't need a theologian for every endeavor. Sometimes a donkey works just fine. 1 Corinthians 1:26-27 says:

> Brothers and sisters, think of what you were when you were called. Not many of you were wise by human standards; not many were influential; not many were of noble birth. But God chose the foolish things of the world to shame the wise; God chose the weak things of the world to shame the strong. (NIV)

If you are a vessel willing to be used, God will use you for his work. I'm satisfied with being the donkey the Lord rides in on.

Jesus said in John 10:27, "My sheep hear my voice, and I know them, and they follow me." (KJV)

If we ask the Lord to reveal His thoughts, He will do exactly that. In fact, the Father has sent the Holy Spirit to be our counselor and teacher. If the Spirit of God is our teacher, we must hear Him. God is reaching out to believers in Christ to heed this warning, draw closer to Him, and strengthen their faith walks.

God is gracious to send many laborers out with warnings for the nation. This is the mercy and love of God telling us ahead of time to turn our hearts back to Him. Some will turn to the Lord with stern verbal warnings, and others will wait for the moment judgment comes upon the land. Sometimes punishment is the only thing that can turn the hardest hearts.

Psalm 9:7-9 says, "The LORD reigns forever; he has established his throne for judgment. He will judge the world in righteousness; he will govern the peoples with justice. The LORD is a refuge for the oppressed, a stronghold in times of trouble." (NIV)

My Story

I am the oldest of four children, born in Southeast Michigan to a Mexican-American mother and a Anglo-American father. Both sides of the family are third and fourth generation, respectively, so they have a long history in the United States. They met when they were seniors in high school and probably not fully ready for the duties of parenthood, but they did their best.

My parents separated five years later, leaving my young mother to care for us. Today, more than 50 percent of children in the United States are from divorced homes. As a result of my parents' separation, we became partially dependent on government aid for a season. We struggled to have a working car and had to go without some of the finer things in life. We received less than $500 a month, but we were never without food and clothing. This experience helped build my faith. God's provision was evident.

I was unhappy with my parents' separation, but my relationship with God filled the empty hole. He is the Father to the fatherless and His Word does not return void. Later, my mom married, and God further restored the family unit in our home.

Trials can birth great faith, and I am grateful for the trials in my life. I understand the struggles of poverty that touch a lot of American families. Most poverty comes from dismantling the family, which leads to dependence on government assistance. Generation after generation ends up on welfare. Families putting their faith in Jesus and less in government handouts can help them break this ugly cycle. The church can walk hand in hand with struggling communities to help restore biblical teaching and provide basic needs. We can contribute to ministries that are making a difference in our areas.

Some of my first encounters with the church of God involved Christian ministries meeting my family's needs. We received gift baskets for Christmas and sometimes Easter. I saw the love not only in the gifts, but also in the faces of the people who delivered them. So, I'm thankful for the laborers who reach out with the love of Christ.

I am far removed from the struggles of poverty today, but I'm thankful that God has used the difficult experiences in my life to keep my heart tender to the needs of others. I try to help as God appoints me to fill a need.

Historically Americans have been generous givers, which may be the reason God has given us so much mercy instead of judgment. According to an article from the *New York Post*:

> … American charitable giving exceeds the entire GDP of most European countries. According to the Almanac of American Philanthropy, Americans donate around seven times as much as continental Europeans to charitable causes per capita.
>
> Every year, six out of ten households in the United States donate to a charitable cause, and the typical household gives somewhere around $2,000 to $3,000.[1]

According to an article in *U.S. News and World Report,* earlier this fall, the World Giving Index ranked the United States as the world's most generous country.[2] This index is annually released by the UK-based nonprofit Charities Aid Foundation and is based on ten years' worth of data

---

1 "Americans are more generous than Europeans — by a large margin," *New York Post* article by David Harsanyi, October 23, 2021. https://nypost.com/2021/10/23/americans-are-more-generous-than-europeans-by-a-large-margin/

2 "Measuring the world's most generous countries," by Sintia Radu, *U.S. News* article, December 20, 2019. https://www.usnews.com/news/best-countries/articles/2019-12-20/the-worlds-most-generous-countries

from annual World Poll surveys by Gallup, the U.S. analytics and advisory firm.

The American people have been given much, which means God requires much in return. Having a giving legacy is the call of Christ and a testament to America's Christian heritage. Deuteronomy 10:18 says, "He executes justice for the fatherless and the widow, and loves the sojourner, giving him food and clothing."

Deuteronomy 14:28-29 says:

> At the end of every three years, bring all the tithes of that year's produce and store it in your towns, so that the Levites (who have no allotment or inheritance of their own) and the foreigners, the fatherless and the widows who live in your towns may come and eat and be satisfied, and so that the Lord your God may bless you in all the work of your hands. (NIV)

And finally, Jesus said in Mathew 25:37-40:

> Then the righteous will answer him, "Lord, when did we see you hungry and feed you, or thirsty and give you something to drink? When did we see you a stranger and invite you in, or needing clothes and clothe you? When did we see you sick or in prison and go to visit you?"

> The King will reply, "Truly I tell you, whatever you did for one of the least of these brothers and sisters of mine, you did for me." (NIV)

The teaching of generosity is deeply rooted in the Christian faith and a requirement under the teachings of Christ.

Finding My Identity in Christ

American identity is shaped much by pop culture and movies. I grew up in the 1980's with movies like "Rocky" and "Karate Kid." These movies portrayed the American spirit, working-class Americans taking on difficult challenges and overcoming against all odds. Our heroes are average people who beat the odds, who overcome adversity.

With God by my side, I thought most anything could be accomplished. I didn't have much financially, but the Bible is full of God's promises, and at a young age, I started to proclaim them over my life.

I excelled at school and sports, eventually winning the National Judo Championship at age twelve. My identity was not shaped by lack; it was shaped by the words of God. This later came to serve me in all aspects of my life. My only wish is that I had hung on every word of truth. I would have saved myself from some of life's pitfalls.

In America, the 80's were a great time. We were absent of war, and anything was possible for those who believed. On the other side of the world, however, people were struggling under communist regimes and even being imprisoned for singing an American song. Eastern Europe was plagued with communism, food shortages, a low quality of life, and an oppressive government.

The torments of these regimes are endless. I heard many first-hand accounts of the effects of communism from my Bulgarian friends. They lost the rights to their property and their children. Everything was owned and controlled by the state. They lived in fear and obedience to corrupt communist/socialist dictators.

I have a friend whose father was a pastor in communist Bulgaria. After a series of encounters with the communist government questioning his faith and giving him electric-shock torture sessions, he decided to flee the country with his young children. The cost of sharing the gospel was high during the era of communism.

The freedoms we have experienced are a gift from above, and we honor the men and women who died to preserve these freedoms and bring equality to all Americans. Galatians 3:28 says, "There is neither Jew nor Greek, there is neither bond nor free, there is neither male nor female; for ye are all one in Christ Jesus." (KJV) The message that all men were created equal with God-given inalienable rights was of primary importance from the Civil War to the Civil Rights Movement. What a blessed message!

While I grew up during a time of prosperity in America, many had forgotten the God of their fathers and replaced the one true God with foreign gods and luxuries. A nation once built on Godly principles had slipped into deep idolatry. It was the beginning of the end of the nation blessed by God.

Our many idols are turning us away from the heart of God and unto our many lovers.

1 Kings 11:3-4 speaks of King Solomon, who loved the true and living God, but whose heart was turned away from Him by his many foreign wives and their idols:

And he had seven hundred wives, princesses, and three hundred concubines: and his wives turned away his heart. For it came to pass, when Solomon was old, that his wives turned away his heart after other gods: and his heart was not perfect with the Lord his God, as was the heart of David his father. (KJV)

Today, many Americans are turned away from the true and living God. Occult practices, witchcraft, and Eastern faith practices are now mainstream in American culture. Our worship of entertainment idols has shifted the nation's cultural and moral climate. Secular culture even tried to remove Christ from Christmas. Our country is in an all-out war against God and the morality of the Bible.

Without God, a nation loses its moral absolutes. What we are experiencing in popular culture today is a result of removing the boundaries that once shaped our society. Without boundaries, even the most taboo practices become commonplace. Sexual immorality, increased crime, and confusion all result from a loss of rules and moral boundaries.

Restoring God to our nation starts heart to heart, on the individual level. Jesus is the author of our hope. Mathew 12:21 says, "In his name the nations will put their hope." (NIV)

My call is a call of repentance to a nation turned away from the one true and living God, the God who gave us freedom, prosperity, and hope for our future.

We are a broken society, but we can be restored by putting our faith and hope in Jesus.

Chapter 2
My Run for Congress

The Lord gave me an urgent warning that laws would to be implemented in America that would limit liberty if more people didn't step forward into a place of government authority. This wave that was coming was a push toward socialism, the promises of which were being peddled like candy to the next generation of young people while the tragedies of this controlling government were being swept over and neglected. People are now looking to the government to pay off student loan debt and medical bills, but dependence on the government means losing important freedoms.

Our freedom was on the line and God prompted me to take a stand.

In Daniel's day, jealous rivals tricked King Darius into issuing a decree that for thirty days no prayers should be addressed to any god or man except Darius himself. Anyone who disobeyed this edict was to be thrown to the lions. Daniel's rivals knew he would break this decree because he was committed to God. Daniel was thrown into the lions' den, and the Lord supernaturally shut the mouths of the lions. This story is documented in Daniel 6:9-11:

> So King Darius signed the edict contained in the written document.
>
> **Daniel is Accused**
>
> When Daniel learned that the written document had been signed, he went to an upstairs room in his house that had windows opened facing Jerusalem. Three times a day he would kneel down, pray, and give thanks to his God, just as he had previously done.
>
> The conspirators then went as a group and found Daniel praying and seeking help before his God. (ISV)

Prior to my run for Congress, I had a series of dreams and encounters that made me aware that the spirit of servitude was slipping into American culture. My first vision showed many American families displaced from their suburban homes and put into government holding camps. Each person was given a number. No one had the right to their own destiny or their own property.

I saw generations of people from multiple nations and ethnicities rise and fall, each of them distinctly in military apparel. I was shown a red book hidden under a pile of kitty litter. When I woke, I asked the Lord, "What does this mean?"

He said to me, "The people represent nations and peoples that have fallen to the sword due to the promises in the red book. The kitty litter represents a coverup. Cat litter covers the smell of animal feces. The new leaders of this movement are trying to cover up the stench of the past horrors of socialism, famines, murder, and servitude. Many people have been persecuted and murdered under the teachings. The little red book represents the philosophy of socialism. Chinese communist leader, Mao, published a red book like this to push socialist propaganda."

At the time of my dream, I was unfamiliar with Mao's red book. This was a further confirmation from the Lord! More than 60 million Chinese citizens were murdered when the Chinese socialist party gained power in China. Landowners were shot and killed, and workers were given part of their property for a time, only to be transferred back to socialist leaders at a later time.

Another dream showed the youth of America dressed in communist apparel, like Fidel Castro, including the beard and mustache. I saw a line of cars in traffic. I looked through my rear window and saw group of youth. I was later shown the same youth dressed in communist apparel. In the dream, I tried to inform them that communism was not cool, hoping they would listen to me.

The cars represented generations, so the car behind mine represented the generation behind me. Every generation wants to represent something big and purposeful, to promote change in some way. The problem begins when we are not taught world history, because history can repeat itself. The road to Hell is paved with good intentions. Good intentions don't neccssarily mean a good outcome.

The first dream followed a chance encounter with two people the next day who had fled communist Bulgaria. Each meeting was separate from the other, and neither person knew the other.

While I was attending a weekly Bible study, I felt the Lord prompt me to share my dream. After doing so, one of the other women in the class said it reminded her of communist Bulgaria. She said when she was a young girl her family had to flee Bulgaria due to political persecution. Her father was a pastor, and the socialist party was targeting him as a nonconformist.

This confirmation alone was enough, but later that day an elderly man walked into my gallery. He complimented the artwork and then told me he was a photographer. He said he was from Bulgaria and had captured many pictures of his people during the communist era. I asked to see his work and the images were riveting. Most of the pictures were taken in the mid-1980's, but the people resembled those from the 1929 Great Depression. He unfolded the story behind each image, and so many brought me to tears. The stories displayed the resilience of the human spirit and the corrupt heart of man when given power over others.

At this point, I knew the Lord was speaking in a clear and tangible way. The spirit of socialism/ communism was coming to America, and I needed to pray and stand against it, or America could end up like Bulgaria. I was willing to do anything the Lord asked, which included spending a significant amount of money to run for Congress.

Bulgaria suffered economic decline after World War II, and the socialist party took its rise because people were desperately seeking help to rebuild their nation.

The Bulgarians elected a socialist government that led to the final legal election in that country. Once the socialists took over, they kept their grip over the people through fraudulent elections all the way to 1989 when their leader was killed.

The Bulgarian people greatly suffered under the socialist regime, and their abundant promises counted for nothing! People were removed from their family properties, wealth was redistributed, and every private business was owned by the government. Thousands of Bulgarians were murdered or sent to labor camps for being nonconformists, wealthy, educated, or threats to the communist system. People lived in fear of speaking against the government because they would either be thrown into a prison camp or put in mental institutions and tortured.

The photographer told me his father spent time in a prison camp and some of his friends were killed by the government. His dream was to come to America where men could be free to speak, free to create, and free to live.

His dreams finally came true after the communist government collapsed in 1989 and he and his family moved to America. After his arrival, however, he was visiting a Detroit library and saw a young American man dressed like Stalin, preaching and sharing books about communism. The photographer thought, *How can this young man be so stupid? Does he not know how many people have suffered and died?* Later, he had a conversation with the young man to straighten out his understanding of the communist system.

The photographer used the terms *socialism* and *communism* interchangeably. He told me there was no difference between the two systems. Socialism was a door to put all the power and resources in the hands of the government and keep them under a communist model. Both systems preach an unattainable utopia at the hands of the government, promises upon promises, all of which lead to death and destruction. Communist regimes are responsible for more than 200 million deaths of their own people worldwide. This is referred to as "death by democide," meaning "death at the hands of your government."

I continued to have further visions of socialism gaining increasing popularity with the youth. So, I committed myself to listen to the voice of the Holy Spirit and run for Congress. I had never been political in nature, though I appreciate the freedoms we have in America, and I have always voted on the national level. But after these alarming dreams and encounters, I wanted to be more forthright. The Lord supernaturally connected me to people who were passionate about freedom, and there was an open seat in my district for a Republican candidate.

I assembled a team and started a campaign. This is probably the most daring thing I have ever done. I never liked speaking in front of people, and I didn't fully know the fight I was about to take on. It was a David and Goliath moment. I knew God was on my side, and that was enough. I stepped forward because He called me. It was a simple act of obedience.

Many people in the party didn't know me, which left room for distrust, negative press, and speculation that I was a spy from the democratic party. But God works everything out for good, and when we are sure God has called us to do something, He is faithful to help. There were so many obstacles in this election, beginning with COVID, which meant all my campaign efforts had to be handled online.

I had to get the signatures I needed to enter the race during a time when no one wanted to meet in person. This meant I couldn't stand in front of the local grocery store and get signatures. We had forced stay-at-home orders in Michigan for nearly a month. Only essential workers could be out.

My team decided to try a campaign that would mail signature requests to the homes of republicans. The team didn't believe we would get a large response, though, because I was an unknown candidate and return mail usually had a low turn-out. I just prayed the people would get the signature requests and return them in time.

While all this was going on, my brother had a dream that reminded him of a scene from the Miracle on 34th Street where the courts were trying to prove the authenticity of Santa Claus. Many letters were sent to courthouses to confirm the man truly was Santa Claus. My brother said in the dream, I was sitting and suddenly mail started rolling in! This confirmed that God was leading people to return the letters with the necessary signatures. And just like that, I received more than 1,500 signatures, which was significantly more than I needed.

So it was official: I was registered to participate in the election. So, I produced a series of videos to help constituents understand the importance of preserving our freedoms. While God's favor was on much of what I did, the opposition was still great.

When I was ahead in the polling, the other candidates attacked me as if we were in a chicken fight, one against three. Accusations against my faith, my sincerity, my family, and my political allegiance were all open for criticism. I forgave everyone who spoke against me, because persecution is usually the price we pay for following Jesus. I didn't expect such an ugly discourse from so many who called themselves followers of Christ. We live in an ugly world, so we need to remain the light.

I ended up winning the walk-in votes for my district but fell short on the mail-in votes. So, I finished as runner-up. Even though I didn't win, I learned that I can do all things through Christ that gives me strength (Philippians 4:13).

As Christ followers, we must be willing to step into the battle wherever He calls us. If He calls you to the mission field, go! If he calls you to the schools, go! If he calls you to the halls of Congress, go! God is with you; you are not alone. He will be glorified even if you fail because He still makes His presence known.

For God's kingdom to advance on earth, His people must be submitted to His will. Scripture is clear that our lives are not our own. We have been bought with a price, and we must live to do the will of God.

Chapter 3
America's Biblical History

Founder John Adams once said, "Our Constitution was made only for a moral and religious people. It is wholly inadequate to the government of any other."[3] Self-government, morality, and Biblical faith are connected, however.

Adams understood that mankind needed civil boundaries. These boundaries are constructed in a moral and religious society to serve as an invisible fence to help keep order. The foundation of this moral code is expressed in the ten commandments. Adams understood that freedom without boundaries leads to loose living which in turn leads to an increase in crime. Eventually, the citizenry will look toward the government to solve their problems. The result is government control and more stringent laws.

The absence of solid moral and religious boundaries, which help clarify convictions and draw lines that keep us from falling into sin, leads to incomplete spiritual lives. Claiming to love Christ is one thing; living in Him is another.

---

3 Barry A. Kosmin and Seymour P. Lachman, *One Nation Under God: Religion in Contemporary American Society* (New York: Harmony Books, 1993), pp. 28–29.

We need boundaries, rules, regulations, and laws to experience true freedom. God does not place those boundaries to test us or to restrict us but to protect us from moral and spiritual calamity, which in turn helps us be good men and women of God.

Our founding fathers were associated with a Christian religious sect, Some may have been better Christians than others, but they all identified as Christians. The point of Adams' statement is that America was not created to be a theocracy but to preserve religious liberty. The First Amendment Bill of Rights says that America was created to be a "beacon of light" to all souls that crave liberty.

According to the book, *One Nation under God: Religion in Contemporary American Society,* by Barry Kosmin, based on the most extensive survey ever conducted on religion in America, "In 1776, every European American, with the exception of about 2,500 Jews, identified himself or herself as a Christian. Moreover, approximately 98 percent of the colonists were Protestants, and the remaining 1.9 percent were Roman Catholics."[4]

Unfortunately, we have allowed a breakdown in our moral standards to the point where we see an increase in lawlessness and debauchery. In the name of modernism, freedom, and liberation, we have removed the moral fence from our schools, making the ten commandments invalid in the eyes of our youth.

---

4 Based on the most extensive survey ever conducted on religion in America, *One Nation Under God* delivers surprising revelations about the religious beliefs, practices, and affiliations of Americans. «These statistical findings provide rich material for interpretation of the uniquely American religious experience.–*Publishers Weekly.*

Even though the law is not our salvation, it does help us create a moral fence. It is a sense of direction and correction for those that have gone astray. 1 Timothy 1:8 says, "We know that the law is good if one uses it properly." (NIV)

We are currently experiencing the results of the secularization of a once-moral and civil society. Many Americans are ready to give up their valuable rights for more government control.

On July 20th, 1956, Americans reaffirmed their moral signpost by adopting resolution 396. This resolution was introduced by Rep. Charles E. Bennet, declared America's national moto to be, "In God We Trust."[5] This is what we must restore "In God we Trust" to reestablish the freedoms all of us should greatly value. This starts with a desire for righteousness and good moral living in the hearts of Americans. Jesus says in Matthew 5:6, in His famous sermon on the mount, "Blessed are those who hunger and thirst for righteousness, for they will be filled." (NIV)

America's modern history starts with the Mayflower Compact, the first document that brought us under a democratic contract as a nation. It contains rules for self-governance written by the English settlers who traveled to the New World on the *Mayflower*[6] 400 years ago in 1620. After sixty-six days at sea, nearly half the crew died on that voyage. The Puritans were deeply religious people who desired to serve God wholeheartedly. After twenty years of persecution in England, they believed God had called them to the New World so they could worship Him

---

5 *America's God and Country Encyclopedia of Quotations*, p. 175, copyright 2017 by William J Feder Amerisearch, Inc.

6 Mayflower Compact. (2009). History. Retrieved from: https://www.history.com/topics/colonial-america/mayflower-compact

in freedom. Once they arrived, they used their God-given wisdom to form a society that combined civil law with biblical views of such freedoms as owning private property, doing business, and educating their children, among other things. They wrote the Mayflower Compact to pioneer this new form of government, and it was signed by forty-one people before they ever got off the ship.

Ever since then, America has been shaped by the values, faith, freedom, and free enterprise of the Puritans.

Since they didn't want a state-operated church that manipulated their freedom to worship as they chose, they constructed a government with a clear separation of church and state. This did not mean they wanted to keep the Bible out of the government and the schools. On the contrary, the Bible had always been the center of all their daily activities.

Throughout the centuries, America has been the promised land for so many seeking a better life. God has graced this land with freedom. Even in our country's darkest hours when slavery was present in the South, the voice of freedom rang louder and truer than the lies of discrimination.

Even though Heaven is the only place without sin, I value the freedoms bestowed upon me by God through this country. As I sit here today, I wonder why so many are ready to give up the freedoms we have for the promises of government servitude. You don't know what you have until it's gone.

In 2021, during the COVID lockdowns, I went to Plymouth Rock to pray for our nation. So, I stood in the place where deeply devoted people of God once stood and asked Him to bring the hearts of Americans back to Him and restore the foundations of our country. God is faithful, and He hears our prayers.

In 1607 Anglican Puritans settled Jamestown, Virginia, and established colleges to help educate future clergy and leaders. These Puritans founded Harvard College in 1636, with a mission statement based on John 17:3 that declared allegiance to God and Jesus Christ: "Everyone shall consider as the main end of his life and studies, to know God and Jesus Christ, which is eternal life."

According to Dr. Roger Schultz, in an article titled, "Christianity and the American University":

> Almost all Ivy League institutions had similar beginnings. They were established by conservative Connecticut Congregationalists (Yale), pro-Awakening New Jersey Presbyterians (Princeton), devout Rhode Island Baptists (Brown), and mission-minded New Hampshire evangelicals (Dartmouth). These schools shared common commitments to the authority of the Word of God, the Gospel of Jesus Christ, and the need for a Christian influence in society.[7]

The deep connection between biblical morality and American education that existed prior to the twentieth century has significantly shifted toward secularism, Darwinism, humanism, and liberalism. As our culture removes God, we will continue to desecrate the moral thread that holds our nation together. Restoring our faith in God will restore the nation we value as home, "In God we Trust."

---

7 "Christianity and the American University," a *Liberty Journal* article by Dr. Roger Schultz, February 26, 2019. https://www.liberty.edu/journal/article/christianity-and-the-american-university/

Chapter 4
A History of Biblical Judgments Among Nations

The Bible is full of stories of those who walked righteously with God and were blessed and those who rejected God's instruction and were cursed. These messages are a roadmap for people and nations to abide in the will and righteousness of God. When nations turn away from God, they turn to idol worship, violence, and rebellion, among other types of sin.

Prophets of old warned such nations of coming judgments and stood as symbols of God's voice in their lands. Some of these prophets performed amazing miracles to shut up the heavens so that no rain fell on the land for years and brought down fire upon the Earth. Today, God is still sending messengers close to His heart to give dreams and visions to the church, and even to babes, of the day of the Lord's judgment.

The revelation God has given me of the coming judgments upon the land has been a progressive one over the

past year. God led me to the book of Nahum, which prophesied the complete destruction of Nineveh, the prideful
capital of Assyria, about 150 years after Jonah delivered
a message of repentance to Nineveh and about fifty-one
years before its fall. At the time the prophecy was written,
Nineveh was at the height of its power and Judah was under
the control of Assyria. During the time of Jonah, Nineveh
repented, and God gave the nation a period of grace.

But there comes a point when God's anger reaches
a tipping point and there is no longer a remedy for our
wounds. Nahum 1:3 says that God is slow to anger, but He
will not leave the guilty unpunished. Nahum 3:4 says that
Nineveh was destroyed because she sold herself to God's
enemies: "All because of the wanton lust of a prostitute,
alluring, the mistress of sorceries, who enslaved nations
by her prostitution and peoples by her witchcraft." (NIV)

I believe America has reached that fatal hour of no return. Our nations has had centuries to repent for our God-
less ways, and we have fallen deeper into sin. Nahum 3:19
discusses what happens when we reach that tipping point
of recompense: "Nothing can heal you; your wound is fatal. All who hear the news about you clap their hands at
your fall, for who has not felt your endless cruelty?"

The soft whisper of the Holy Spirit spoke ever so clearly to me to be a watchman and to warn of coming events.
Ezekiel 33:1-6 says:

> The word of the Lord came to me: "Son of man,
> speak to your people and say to them: 'When I
> bring the sword against a land, and the people of
> the land choose one of their men and make him
> their watchman, and he sees the sword coming

against the land and blows the trumpet to warn the people, then if anyone hears the trumpet but does not heed the warning and the sword comes and takes their life, their blood will be on their own head. Since they heard the sound of the trumpet but did not heed the warning, their blood will be on their own head. If they had heeded the warning, they would have saved themselves. But if the watchman sees the sword coming and does not blow the trumpet to warn the people and the sword comes and takes someone's life, that person's life will be taken because of their sin, but I will hold the watchman accountable for their blood.' (NIV)

Any time the Lord gives us a message, we are accountable for what we know. In my commitment to the Lord, I release this message to prepare for a season of biblical judgments and invite you to renew your heart before the Lord. Psalm 33:12-19 says:

Blessed is the nation whose God is the Lord, the people he chose for his inheritance. From heaven the Lord looks down and sees all mankind; from his dwelling place he watches all who live on Earth—he who forms the hearts of all, who considers everything they do. No king is saved by the size of his army; no warrior escapes by his great strength. A horse is a vain hope for deliverance; despite all its great strength it cannot save. But the eyes of the Lord are on those who fear him, on those whose hope is in his unfailing love, to deliver them from death and keep them alive in famine. (NIV)

God gave me a spiritual confirmation when I was nearing the end of writing this book. I have an art gallery
and ministry in Dallas, Texas. For several days, swarms of
grasshoppers were entering the gallery as we opened the
front door every morning. One morning, a grasshopper
had found its way to my office and jumped in my teacup
for a nap.

I asked the Lord if the grasshoppers were a sign of
something. The Holy Spirit referred me to the locusts in
the Bible. Like grasshoppers, they are a sign of famine
and judgment. I asked the Lord to remove the grasshoppers, and the next day, two birds were standing guard near
my front door. As the grasshoppers approached the door,
the birds quickly ate them.

The following week a distressed homeless man had
stopped to rest near my front door. A few Christians who
saw the distressed man stopped to help him, and I joined
with them in prayer. Later I invited the whole group into
the gallery. The man had a small plastic bag containing all
his belongings. He pulled out a small blue metal cup and
gave it to me as a gift. I thanked him, but I thought it was
strange for him to give me a blue metal cup.

The grasshopper sitting in my cup quickly came to
mind, and I thought God may have been trying to give
me a message. So, I asked God and He gave me the
message He had originally given to the prophet Jeremiah about a sign of coming judgment. I heard the Holy
Spirit whisper Jeremiah 25:17: "So I took the cup from
the Lord's hand and made all the nations to whom he
sent me drink it." (NIV)

The cup the Lord had given Jeremiah was a sign of
God's wrath coming to the nations. God told Jeremiah to

take this cup to the leaders of these nations as a warning. So, the blue cup confirmed the message the Lord had bestowed upon me, that judgment was coming to America and various other nations.

Psalm 46:10 says that God is still on the throne. He is always present and ready to help us whenever we need Him in times of prosperity and in times of judgment. We should never doubt His power and His love for us. No matter what is happening in the world, peace, judgment, and protection are all in His hands, and He does everything in His time.

God is all-knowing. Whether we're talking loudly or not saying anything, God is still looking down upon His creation. Sometimes bad things happen because God wants us to become stronger, more resilient, and more dependent on Him, but He is always working out great things for us.

The nation of Israel, the "Apple of God's eye," a nation set apart for God's purpose, was blessed during the reign of King David and continued to be blessed under King Solomon. God had separated Israel as a holy priesthood. This special relationship came with a special blessing or curse depending on the Israelites' willingness to follow the Mosaic Law, which was a witness to the holiness of God.

The Bible says that God loves Israel "forever," but as Israel's kings began to turn away from God's holy commandments, God took their blessing away and eventually exiled them to Babylon.

Chapter 5
Abundant Blessing Can Lead to Gluttony and Forgetfulness

God warned Israel in Deuteronomy 8:6-20 not to forget God in their blessing:

> Observe the commands of the Lord your God, walking in obedience to him and revering him. For the Lord your God is bringing you into a good land—a land with brooks, streams, and deep springs gushing out into the valleys and hills; a land with wheat and barley, vines and fig trees, pomegranates, olive oil and honey; a land where bread will not be scarce, and you will lack nothing; a land where the rocks are iron and you can dig copper out of the hills.

> When you have eaten and are satisfied, praise the Lord your God for the good land he has given you. Be careful that you do not forget the Lord your

God, failing to observe his commands, his laws and his decrees that I am giving you this day. Otherwise, when you eat and are satisfied, when you build fine houses and settle down, and when your herds and flocks grow large and your silver and gold increase and all you have is multiplied, then your heart will become proud and you will forget the Lord your God, who brought you out of Egypt, out of the land of slavery. He led you through the vast and dreadful wilderness, that thirsty and waterless land, with its venomous snakes and scorpions. He brought you water out of hard rock. He gave you manna to eat in the wilderness, something your ancestors had never known, to humble and test you so that in the end it might go well with you. You may say to yourself, "My power and the strength of my hands have produced this wealth for me." But remember the Lord your God, for it is he who gives you the ability to produce wealth, and so confirms his covenant, which he swore to your ancestors, as it is today.

If you ever forget the Lord your God and follow other gods and worship and bow down to them, I testify against you today that you will surely be destroyed. Like the nations the Lord destroyed before you, so you will be destroyed for not obeying the Lord your God. (NIV)

God was preparing to bring them into a land flowing with milk and honey, the abundant life. But King Solomon's marriages to wives who worshipped other gods brought idols into the land, which weakened the king's commitment to the God of Jacob. God had given Solomon great riches, but the opulence in his life led his heart astray. His son, Rehoboam, succeeded him on the throne, but his desire for power was greater than his desire to serve God, as his attempt to rule Israel with an iron rod divided the Promised Land.

America once had the same commitment to God, and the rest of the world has profited from the flourishing of our great nation. God has given us the blessing of freedom and a Constitution that makes it firm, but our prosperity has moved our hearts away from worshipping the God of the Bible to worshipping the bull of the marketplace. Our desire to make more money so we can buy more things has led to worshipping luxury, materialism, entertainment, and sports, among other things, which leaves little time to worship the true and living God. Our idols may look different from Israel's, but they are the same in God's eyes.

Abundance and excess have led to the rise of superstores like Walmart and Target, which in turn have led to many Americans losing their businesses to overseas companies and manufacturers. We have even compromised our freedoms to trade with communist nations, which has led to serious debt. According to an article titled, "How Much U.S. Debt Does China Own?" as of January 2022, the United States owes China approximately $1.06 trillion.[8] In addition, excessive government spending during COVID has pushed education, housing, and food prices higher. As of February 2022, our national debt is $30 trillion.

---

8 "How Much U.S. Debt Does China Own?" by the *Investopedia* team, July 24, 2022. https://www.investopedia.com/articles/investing/080615/china-owns-us-debt-how-much.asp

According to a 2021 CNBC report, the average American has $90,460 in debt. That included credit cards, personal loans, mortgages, and student debt.[9] As of 2020, Gen Z (ages 18 to 23) carries an average debt of $16,043; Millennials (ages 24 to 39) carry an average debt of $87,448; Gen X (ages 40 to 55) carries an average debt of $140,643; Baby Boomers (ages 56 to 74) carry an average debt of $97,290; and the Silent Generation (ages 75 and above) carries an average debt of $41,281.

Lavish lifestyles are also admired in the church, as many pastors preach more about earthly prosperity than repentance and salvation. In Matthew 6:24, however, Jesus reminds His "church" that we can't love both God and money: "No one can serve two masters. Either you will hate the one and love the other, or you will be devoted to the one and despise the other. You cannot serve both God and money." (NIV)

Jeremiah 10:8-16 warned Israel that the worship of idols would bring destruction upon the land. It will also bring destruction upon ours:

> People who worship idols are stupid and foolish. The things they worship are made of wood! They bring beaten sheets of silver from Tarshish and gold from Uphaz, and they give these materials to skillful craftsmen who make their idols. Then they dress these gods in royal blue and purple robes made by expert tailors. But the Lord is the only true God. He is the living God and the everlasting King! The whole earth trembles at his

9 "Demographics of Debt," by Bill Fay, February 23, 2022. https://www. debt.org/faqs/americans-in-debt/demographics/

anger. The nations cannot stand up to his wrath. Say this to those who worship other gods: "Your so-called gods, who did not make the heavens and earth, will vanish from the earth and from under the heavens." (NLT)

Chapter 6
A Word for the Nation

God is calling America to turn back to honoring Him in word and deed.

The Lord gave me a dream about the coming judgment and continues to provoke my spirit to the urgency of the hour. I saw a time of great chaos and desperation. People were acting like animals, violent and without compassion. The Holy Spirit urged me to fast that day because He wanted to speak to me more clearly.

The Lord continues to say to me that the judgment of God, a great shaking, is coming to our nation. I received this message as a waking word from the Lord: "I no longer feel pity on this nation." The word had a deep emptiness and sorrow, as though the sin of the nation has reached its tipping point and God has had enough.

I asked God if He had used the same words in scripture, and I saw them echoed in Ezekiel 7:5-9:

> This is what the Sovereign Lord says: "Disaster! Unheard-of disaster! See, it comes! The end has come!

The end has come! It has roused itself against you. See, it comes! Doom has come upon you, upon you who dwell in the land. The time has come! The day is near! There is panic, not joy, on the mountains. I am about to pour out my wrath on you and spend my anger against you. I will judge you according to your conduct and repay you for all your detestable practices. <u>I will not look on you with pity; I will not spare you</u>. I will repay you for your conduct and for the detestable practices among you. (NIV, emphasis mine)

I believe God is saying His grace and mercy have reached the tipping point and that judgment is upon us because He no longer feels remorse for our nation. We have turned so far into sin, idolatry, and paganism that the Lord has lifted His hand of protection.

We have lived in abundance only because of the grace of God upon our land, but the hearts of the people are far removed from the will of the Lord. The foundation of this nation is deeply cracked, like the crack in the liberty bell. The bell of liberty is slipping away and only God's mercy can restore us.

Former President Kennedy had planned to quote Psalm 127 in a speech prior to his death in Dallas on November 22, 1963: "Unless the Lord builds the house, those who build it labor in vain. Unless the Lord watches over the city, the watchman stays awake in vain." This verse rings even more true today than it did then. We need God's protection and favour upon our land, or the watchman watches in vain. Following is an excerpt from the rest of the speech:

We in this country, in this generation, are—by destiny rather than choice—the watchmen on the walls of world freedom. We ask, therefore, that we may be worthy of our power and responsibility, that we may exercise our strength with wisdom and restraint, and that we may achieve in our time and for all time the ancient vision of "Peace on earth, good will toward men." That must always be our goal, and the righteousness of our cause must underlie our strength.

Kennedy described America as "watchmen on the walls of world freedom." Many today would like to keep this important international role, but others are willing to give it up along with their own freedoms for a false sense of security at the hands of the government.

President Ronald Reagan continued the fight for world freedom during his presidency. He negotiated the end of the Cold War and the removal of the Berlin Wall separating Eastern and Western Germany during the era of communism. He warned Americans that freedom must be fought for and preserved for future generations. Freedom is not a norm. Many nations have suffered under brutal dictators. Reagan also warned that freedom once lost would be nearly impossible to restore:

Freedom is never more than one generation away from extinction. We didn't pass it to our children in the bloodstream. It must be fought for, protected, and handed on for them to do the same, or one day we will spend our sunset years telling our children and our children's children what it was once like in the United States where men were free.[10]

10 https://www.reagan.com/ronald-reagan-freedom-speech

On July 7, 1775, John Adams wrote similar sentiments in a letter to his wife, Abigail: "Liberty once lost is lost forever. When the People once surrender their share in the Legislature, and their Right of defending the Limitations upon the Government, and of resisting every Encroachment upon them, they can never regain it."

American prosperity has led to American idolatry. Generation after generation does not fully understand that this nation was created for the freedom to worship God as we will, not to remove God from the public and private sector. We have failed to teach our children our history, and our wealth has added to our spiritual independence from God.

We have even allowed the Bible, the most widely read book in the world, to be banned from many public school districts. A CBS news article by Penny Starr titled, "Education Expert: Removing Bible, Prayer from Public Schools Has Caused Decline," reads:

> On June 25, 1962, the United States Supreme Court decided in Engel v. Vitale that a prayer approved by the New York Board of Regents for use in schools violated the First Amendment because it represented establishment of religion. In 1963, in Abington School District v. Schempp, the court decided against Bible readings in public schools along the same lines.[11]

---

11 "Education Expert: Removing Bible, Prayer from Public Schools Has Caused Decline," by Penny Starr, August 15, 2014. https://www.cnsnews.com/news/article/penny-starr/education expert-removing-bible-prayer-public-schools-has-caused-decline

In 1984, former President Ronald Regan expounded on the removal of prayer in public schools while giving a speech as the Ecumenical Prayer Breakfast at Reunion Arena in Dallas, Texas.

In 1962, the Supreme Court in New York prayer case banned the.. saying of prayers. In 1963, the Court banned the reading of the Bible in our public schools. From that point on, the courts pushed the meaning of the ruling outward, so that now our children are not allowed voluntary prayer.

We even had to pass a law—pass a special law in the Congress just a few weeks ago – to allow student prayer groups the same access to school rooms after classes that a Young Marxist Society, for example, would already enjoy with no opposition...

The 1962 decision opened the way to a flood of similar suits. Once religion had been made vulnerable, a series of assaults were made in one court after another, one issue after another.

Cases were started to argue the tax-exempt status for churches. Suits were brought to abolish the words "Under God" from the Pledge of Allegiance, and to remove "In God We Trust" from public documents and from our currency.

Without God there is no virtue because there is no prompting of conscience... without God there is a coarsening of the society; without God democracy will not and cannot endure... If we ever forget that we are One Nation Under God, then we will be a nation gone under.[12]

---

12 *America's God and Country Encyclopedia of Quotations* p. 529-530 copyright 2017 by William J Feder Amerisearch, Inc.

The removal of the Bible from public arena has left a hole in the hearts of the American people. Mankind is spiritual in nature, our need to pray and seek a higher wisdom and spiritual fulfillment has been filled with the occult, the worship of stones and a reliance on foreign faiths and pharmaceuticals.

King David was extremely wealthy, but his heart was to serve the Lord first. His son, Solomon, started out with a heart to please God, but later turned from Him to worshipping idols. 1 Kings 11:4-6 says that Solomon's many wives turned his heart away from the Lord:

> As Solomon grew old, his wives turned his heart after other gods, and his heart was not fully devoted to the Lord his God, as the heart of David his father had been. He followed Ashtoreth the goddess of the Sidonians, and Molek the detestable god of the Ammonites. So Solomon did evil in the eyes of the Lord; he did not follow the Lord completely, as David his father had done. (NIV)

Are there idols in our own lives that are turning our hearts away from the Lord? Do you spend more time watching Netflix and primetime sports than reading the Word of God? Have the luxuries in your life become idols? Do we worship the gift more than the Giver? It is our human nature to become complacent, but idolatry can weaken our walk with the Lord and quickly lead us astray.

God is judging the altar to Baal in our nation and bringing His justice to our land. We have recently seen this judgment with the overturn of Roe vs. Wade and the destruction of the Georgia Guidestones, commonly known as America's Stonehenge. This monument purported to kill 90 percent of the world's population through eugenics, faith centered on reason, and world government.

On July 6th, 2022, an explosion happened and this standing monument was destroyed. Its destruction brought this long-standing structure back in the news and the guidance this monument was offering humanity:

1. Maintain humanity under 500,000,000 in perpetual balance with nature.
2. Guide reproduction wisely — improving fitness and diversity.
3. Unite humanity with a living new language.
4. Rule passion — faith — tradition — and all things with tempered reason.
5. Protect people and nations with fair laws and just courts.
6. Let all nations rule internally, resolving external disputes in a world court.
7. Avoid petty laws and useless officials.
8. Balance personal rights with social duties.
9. Prize truth — beauty — love — seeking harmony with the infinite.
10. Be not a cancer on the Earth — Leave room for nature.

Clearly the most shocking statement in this written decree is the suggested massive reduction in world population. Our current population is just under 8 billion, and in 1980, when the stones were erected, the population was 4.4 billion, so the recommendation of a 500-million-person reduction, is nearly an 80 percent decrease from 1980's world population. Only a massive catastrophe or a mass genocide could decrease the planet by such numbers.

Number 2 on the list speaks of guiding production wisely, I assume via some type of production protocol or laws. This is a viewpoint that eugenicists like Adolf Hitler and founder of Planned Parenthood, Margaret Sanger, subscribed to. They wanted to guide reproduction to eliminate people groups they saw as inferior.

Margret Sanger was an occultist connected to the Masonic Order and Lucis Trust, a prominent modern-day representative of Theosophy, an extension of the Lucifer Publishing Company, which is also a United Nations NGO. Lucis Trust was founded by Alice A. Bailey, a nominal leader of the Theosophical Society in the early 1900s. Both Sanger and Hitler were involved in a religion that worshipped Lucifer and were energized by the same dark, spiritual forces.

Publications from Lucis Trust regularly refer to "The Plan" for humanity that has been established by "The Hierarchy." Sanger's disciples are alive and functioning today, influencing national and international population control policy. Sanger believed ethnic races were inferior and in creating a superior race of people. According to *Woman's Body, Woman's Right,* by Linda Gordon:

In 1939, Margaret Sanger organized the *Negro Project,* designed to eliminate members of what she believed to be an "inferior race." She justified her proposal because "the masses of Negroes... particularly in the South, still breed carelessly and disastrously, with the result that the increase among Negroes, even more than among whites, is from that portion of the population least intelligent and fit...."[13]

---

13 *Woman's Body, Woman's Right,* Linda Gordon, Penguin Press, New York,

We can also look at China's one-child policy implemented between 1980 and 2015 as a means of controlling reproduction. Young women were forced into sterilization and heavy surveillance after having one child. They faced large fines for noncompliance and abortion was mandatory in many cases. Male children were prioritized under this policy, and many unwanted baby girls in China were left for dead or given up for adoption outside the country. The Chinese communist government sees this policy as a great success as would many of our current scientific thinkers.

Number 3 on the list advocates for the reestablishment of the Tower of Babel, bringing everyone under a common language. This command is act of rebellion against God's Word, as it's mankind's attempt to build its own kingdom.

Number 4 is an attempt to reduce religious zeal and elevate reason over faith.

Number 6 advocates for a world government.

Number 7 is vague, but the words "petty" and "useless" will be decided by an elite class that undervalues human life.

Number 8 proposes we limit our personal liberty for government agendas.

And number 10 is the New Age environmentalist and globalist elevating Mother Earth above mankind.

Georgia Guidestones was approximately 666 miles from UN Headquarters. My point-to-point calculation revealed 666.66 miles between the two locations. The picture below shows a screenshot of my calculation at 9:11pm. Some people believe this revelation links the Guidestones

p. 332; see also *Killer Angel,* p. 73.

to the global government initiatives and the coming mark of beast in Revelation 13:16-18:

> And he causeth all, both small and great, rich and poor, free and bond, to receive a mark in their right hand, or in their foreheads: And that no man might buy or sell, save he that had the mark, or the name of the beast, or the number of his name. Here is wisdom. Let him that hath understanding count the number of the beast: for it is the number of a man; and his number is Six hundred threescore and six. (KJV)

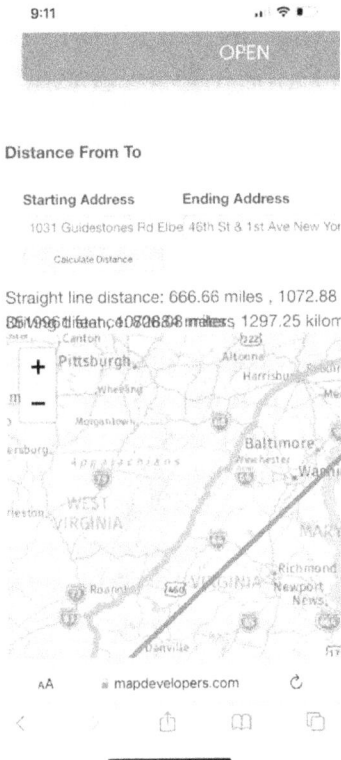

The bottom line is that every altar lifted to a false god will be destroyed and altars to the God of Heaven will be erected. God gave me the word, "American Pharaoh." Since its inception, America has lifted up the true God and false gods, but God is separating the wheat from the chaff. He will judge the false gods along with those who worship them, and the true God will be exalted. Just as God judged the Egyptian gods in the days of Pharaoh, acts of judgment will come upon our land.

As Christians, we need to flee from the worship of false gods, the worship of men, the worship of anything other than the true and living God, embodied in the person of Jesus Christ.

Chapter 7
Blessings and Curses

If we want to achieve success, we need to do what God commands us to do. Deuteronomy 28 discusses the blessings we receive when we follow God and warns us of the consequences when we fail to obey Him.

Blessings for Obedience

If you fully obey the Lord your God and carefully follow all his commands I give you today, the Lord your God will set you high above all the nations on Earth. All these blessings will come on you and accompany you if you obey the Lord your God: You will be blessed in the city and blessed in the country. The fruit of your womb will be blessed, and the crops of your land and the young of your livestock—the calves of your herds and the lambs of your flocks. Your basket and your kneading trough will be blessed. You will be blessed when you come in and blessed when you go out. The Lord will grant that the enemies who rise up against you will be defeated before you. They will come at you from one direction but flee from you in seven. The Lord will send a blessing on your barns and on everything you put your hand to. The Lord your God will bless you in the land he is giving you.

The Lord will establish you as his holy people, as he promised you on oath, if you keep the commands of the Lord your God and walk in obedience to him. Then all the peoples on Earth will see that you are called by the name of the Lord, and they will fear you. The Lord will grant you abundant prosperity—in the fruit of your womb, the young of your livestock and the crops of your ground—in the land he swore to your ancestors to give you.

The Lord will open the heavens, the storehouse of his bounty, to send rain on your land in season and to bless all the work of your hands. You will lend to many nations but will borrow from none. The Lord will make you the head, not the tail. If you pay attention to the commands of the Lord your God that I give you this day and carefully follow them, you will always be at the top, never at the bottom. Do not turn aside from any of the commands I give you today, to the right or to the left, following other gods and serving them.

Curses for Disobedience

However, if you do not obey the Lord your God and do not carefully follow all his commands and decrees I am giving you today, all these curses will come on you and overtake you: You will be cursed in the city and cursed in the country. Your basket and your kneading trough will be cursed. The fruit of your womb will be cursed, and the crops of your land, and the calves of your herds and the lambs of your flocks. You will be cursed when you come in and cursed when you go out.

The Lord will send on you curses, confusion and rebuke in everything you put your hand to, until you are destroyed and come to sudden ruin because of the evil you have done in forsaking him. The Lord will plague you with diseases until he has destroyed you from the land you are entering to possess. The Lord will strike you with wasting disease, with fever and inflammation, with scorching heat and drought, with blight and mildew, which will plague you until you perish. The sky over your head will be bronze, the ground beneath you iron. The Lord will turn the rain of your country into dust and powder; it will come down from the skies until you are destroyed.

The Lord will cause you to be defeated before your enemies. You will come at them from one direction but flee from them in seven, and you will become a thing of horror to all the kingdoms on Earth. Your

carcasses will be food for all the birds and the wild
animals, and there will be no one to frighten them
away. The Lord will afflict you with the boils of
Egypt and with tumors, festering sores and the itch,
from which you cannot be cured. The Lord will afflict you with madness, blindness and confusion of
mind. At midday you will grope about like a blind
person in the dark. You will be unsuccessful in everything you do; day after day you will be oppressed
and robbed, with no one to rescue you.

You will be pledged to be married to a woman, but
another will take her and rape her. You will build
a house, but you will not live in it. You will plant a
vineyard, but you will not even begin to enjoy its
fruit. Your ox will be slaughtered before your eyes,
but you will eat none of it. Your donkey will be forc-
ibly taken from you and will not be returned. Your
sheep will be given to your enemies, and no one will
rescue them. Your sons and daughters will be given
to another nation, and you will wear out your eyes
watching for them day after day, powerless to lift a
hand. A people that you do not know will eat what
your land and labor produce, and you will have
nothing but cruel oppression all your days. The
sights you see will drive you mad. The Lord will afflict your knees and legs with painful boils that cannot be cured, spreading from the soles of your feet
to the top of your head.

The Lord will drive you and the king you set over
you to a nation unknown to you or your ances-

tors. There you will worship other gods, gods of wood and stone. You will become a thing of horror, a byword and an object of ridicule among all the peoples where the Lord will drive you.

You will sow much seed in the field but you will harvest little, because locusts will devour it. You will plant vineyards and cultivate them but you will not drink the wine or gather the grapes, because worms will eat them. You will have olive trees throughout your country but you will not use the oil, because the olives will drop off. You will have sons and daughters but you will not keep them, because they will go into captivity. Swarms of locusts will take over all your trees and the crops of your land.

The foreigners who reside among you will rise above you higher and higher, but you will sink lower and lower. They will lend to you, but you will not lend to them. They will be the head, but you will be the tail.

All these curses will come on you. They will pursue you and overtake you until you are destroyed, because you did not obey the Lord your God and observe the commands and decrees he gave you. They will be a sign and a wonder to you and your descendants forever. Because you did not serve the Lord your God joyfully and gladly in the time of prosperity, therefore in hunger and thirst, in nakedness and dire poverty, you will serve the enemies the Lord sends against you. He will put an iron yoke on your neck until he has destroyed you.

The Lord will bring a nation against you from far away, from the ends of the Earth, like an eagle swooping down, a nation whose language you will not understand, a fierce-looking nation without respect for the old or pity for the young. They will devour the young of your livestock and the crops of your land until you are destroyed. They will leave you no grain, new wine or olive oil, nor any calves of your herds or lambs of your flocks until you are ruined. They will lay siege to all the cities throughout your land until the high fortified walls in which you trust fall down. They will besiege all the cities throughout the land the Lord your God is giving you.

Because of the suffering your enemy will inflict on you during the siege, you will eat the fruit of the womb, the flesh of the sons and daughters the Lord your God has given you. Even the most gentle and sensitive man among you will have no compassion on his own brother or the wife he loves or his surviving children, and he will not give to one of them any of the flesh of his children that he is eating. It will be all he has left because of the suffering your enemy will inflict on you during the siege of all your cities. The most gentle and sensitive woman among you—so sensitive and gentle that she would not venture to touch the ground with the sole of her foot—will begrudge the husband she loves and her own son or daughter the afterbirth from her womb and the children she bears. For in her dire need she intends to eat them secretly because of the suffering your enemy will inflict on you during the siege of your cities.

If you do not carefully follow all the words of this law, which are written in this book, and do not revere this glorious and awesome name— the Lord your God— the Lord will send fearful plagues on you and your descendants, harsh and prolonged disasters, and severe and lingering illnesses. He will bring on you all the diseases of Egypt that you dreaded, and they will cling to you. The Lord will also bring on you every kind of sickness and disaster not recorded in this Book of the Law, until you are destroyed. You who were as numerous as the stars in the sky will be left but few, because you did not obey the Lord your God. Just as it pleased the Lord to make you prosper and increase in number, so it will please him to ruin and destroy you. You will be uprooted from the land you are entering to possess.

Then the Lord will scatter you among all nations, from one end of the Earth to the other. There you will worship other gods—gods of wood and stone, which neither you nor your ancestors have known. Among those nations you will find no repose, no resting place for the sole of your foot. There the Lord will give you an anxious mind, eyes weary with longing, and a despairing heart. You will live in constant suspense, filled with dread both night and day, never sure of your life. In the morning you will say, "If only it were evening!" and in the evening, "If only it were morning!"—because of the terror that will fill your hearts and the sights that your eyes will see. The Lord will send you back in ships to Egypt on a journey I said you should never make again. There you will offer yourselves for sale to your enemies as male and female slaves, but no one will buy you. (NIV)

These curses and blessings were fully realized at different points in Israel's history. Deuteronomy 28:64-65 foretells the exile of the Israelites from their homeland as a result of their rebellion against God:

Then the Lord will scatter you among all nations, from one end of the Earth to the other. There you will worship other gods—gods of wood and stone, which neither you nor your ancestors have known. Among those nations you will find no repose, no resting place for the sole of your foot. (NIV)

The prophets later revealed that God would restore Israel and bring them back to the land of their forefathers. Jeremiah 29:10 talks about the first return of Jews to their homeland after seventy years in Babylon: "This is what the Lord says: "When seventy years are completed for Babylon, I will come to you and fulfill my good promise to bring you back to this place." (NIV)

Isaiah 11:11-12 speaks of another return of Jews gathering from the ends of the earth, which many in our generation have witnessed:

> In that day the Lord will reach out his hand a second time to reclaim the surviving remnant of his people from Assyria, from Lower Egypt, from Upper Egypt, from Cush, from Elam, from Babylonia, from Hamath and from the islands of the Mediterranean. He will raise a banner for the nations and gather the exiles of Israel; he will assemble the scattered people of Judah from the four quarters of the Earth. (NIV)

God also judges those that rebel against Him. In the days of Noah, for example, God looked down upon His creation and He was sad that He had created mankind because of all of its wickedness. Genesis 6:5-7 describes how He sent a great flood from heaven that came down and covered the whole earth, killing everyone except Noah's family, the only people God judged to be righteous, and the animals. God told Noah to build an ark, measuring approximately 400 feet long x 300 feet wide, and to board the ark, along with his family, and two of every kind of animal:

> Then the LORD saw that the wickedness of man was great upon the Earth, and that every inclination of the thoughts of his heart was altogether evil all the time. And the LORD regretted that He had made man on the Earth, and He was grieved in His heart. So the LORD said, "I will blot out man, whom I have created, from the face of the earth—every man and beast and crawling creature and bird of the air—for I am grieved that I have made them. (BSB)

God also judged Sodom and Gomorrah for their wickedness, as revealed in Genesis 19:12-13:

> The two men said to Lot, "Do you have anyone
> else here—sons-in-law, sons or daughters, or any-
> one else in the city who belongs to you? Get them
> out of here, because we are going to destroy this
> place. The outcry to the LORD against its people is
> so great that he has sent us to destroy it." (NIV)

The book of Exodus reveals that Egypt was one of
the first nations God judged for refusing to allow the
Israelites to leave captivity. God brought ten plagues
upon their land. The final plague was the death of all
the first-born sons.

The prophets later prophesied the coming judgment
upon the nations. In Ezekiel 12:3-6, God instructed the
prophet Ezekiel to act out Israel's exile to Babylon, demon-
strating how God would judge the Israelites:

> Therefore, son of man, pack your belongings for ex-
> ile and in the daytime, as they watch, set out and go
> from where you are to another place. Perhaps they
> will understand, though they are a rebellious peo-
> ple. During the daytime, while they watch, bring
> out your belongings packed for exile. Then in the
> evening, while they are watching, go out like those
> who go into exile. While they watch, dig through the
> wall and take your belongings out through it. Put
> them on your shoulder as they are watching and
> carry them out at dusk. Cover your face so that you

cannot see the land, for I have made you a sign to the Israelites. (NIV)

Isaiah 13:11 prophesies the coming judgment upon Babylon: "I will punish the world for its evil, the wicked for their sins. I will put an end to the arrogance of the haughty and will humble the pride of the ruthless." (NKJV)

Isaiah 14:24-27 prophesies the coming judgment on Assyria:

> The Lord Almighty has sworn, "Surely, as I have planned, so it will be, and as I have purposed, so it will happen. I will crush the Assyrian in my land; on my mountains I will trample him down. His yoke will be taken from my people, and his burden removed from their shoulders." This is the plan determined for the whole world; this is the hand stretched out over all nations. For the Lord Almighty has purposed, and who can thwart him? (NIV)

Isaiah 23:1-9 prophesies the coming judgment on Tyre:

> Wail, you ships of Tarshish! For Tyre is destroyed and left without house or harbor. From the land of Cyprus word has come to them. Be silent, you people of the island and you merchants of Sidon, whom the seafarers have enriched. On the great waters came the grain of the Shihor; the harvest of the Nile was the revenue of Tyre, and she became the marketplace of the nations. Be ashamed, Sidon, and you fortress of the sea, for the sea has spoken: "I have neither been in labor nor given

birth; I have neither reared sons nor brought up daughters." When word comes to Egypt, they will be in anguish at the report from Tyre. Cross over to Tarshish; wail, you people of the island. Is this your city of revelry, the old, old city, whose feet have taken her to settle in far-off lands? Who planned this against Tyre, the bestower of crowns, whose merchants are princes, whose traders are renowned in the earth? The LORD Almighty planned it, to bring down her pride in all her splendor and to humble all who are renowned on the earth. (NIV)

As we can see from reading the text, pride, wickedness, haughtiness, and idolatry were the reasons God brought judgment upon the nations.

The book of Jonah, on the other hand, displays God's mercy when people repent from their sin. But before Jonah could share that message with the Ninevites, he had to repent of his own sin of trying to get away from sharing God's message and ending up in the belly of a big fish. Once Jonah repented and shared the message with the Ninevites, the entire nation, including the livestock, repented and fasted for three days without water.

As a result of this temporary sacrifice of true repentance, God relented from judging Nineveh for nearly ninety years. Unfortunately, a future generation of Ninevites went back to their old ways, and Nahum sent a new prophecy of certain judgment upon the nation. Since then, Nineveh has ceased to exist as the vibrant civilization it once was.

Simply put, God's judgment is a symbol of God's justice. He is a holy and perfect Creator who brings justice to the earth in its due season. The all-knowing nature of God sees the injustice, the murder, and the abuse that has occurred over the centuries and is still occurring at this present hour. He hears the prayers and cries from the saints calling out for His righteous justice and, as Job 34:11 declares, "He repays everyone for what they have done; he brings on them what their conduct deserves." (NIV)

Chapter 8
America's Dual Identity

America is a land known for freedom and prosperity, rich in natural resources. It has been the promised land for many all over the world fleeing totalitarian governments, but is America all she reveals herself to be?

On one hand, America was founded by a group of Christians fleeing religious persecution (the aforementioned Puritans), and on the other hand, some of America's founders were members of secret occult orders with their own agendas. While the Puritans wanted to live peaceably with the Native Americans and share their faith with the tribes, others had plans to profit off the land, take its territory, and import slaves.

This dual spirituality is evident if we look closely at the hidden symbols printed on our money. To some, "In God We Trust," which is stamped on our money, means the biblical God, and to others it means the "God of this World" (aka Lucifer, also known as the eye of Horus, also known as Apollo or Osiris).

The text underneath the pyramid, "Novis Ordo Seclorum," translates "A New Order of the Ages."

While America has elected officials who place their hand on the Bible to take an oath of office, is full of churches and Christian schools, and has sent more missionaries to preach the gospel than any other country in history, even our first president, George Washington was a member of the Masons. The Masons link themselves to ancient occult rituals, goddess worship, and even Lucifer worship. The Masonic Order known as the Scottish Rite, which has a powerful place in the founding of our nation and political climate, also has connections to the Illuminati.

Much like the Puritans, the Masons and the Illuminati were looking for a new land to worship freely. The Illuminati had a falling out with the Catholic Church when a written plan was revealed to destroy the church and bring in a global government that would overthrow the monarchy. This forced many faithful members of the Illuminati to the New World.

According to the book, *Masons Who Shaped Our Nation*, written by Freemasons, [14] twenty-three of the thirty-nine patriots who signed the Constitution were brothers of the craft. The book also reveals that President Washington ap-

---

14 *Masons Who Shaped Our Nation* by Freemasons, p. 84. Copyright 1976, Neyenesch Printers.

pointed four Freemasons to the Supreme Court, and as of 1976, thirty-five of the ninety-six justices were Masons.

Many of our founders attended church frequently, but some were also deists, which means they believed God created the earth, but didn't actively engage in the daily activities of mankind. Their search for God was connected to a pattern of good works that would ultimately memorialize man himself. The Masonic Order cloaks itself in good deeds and philanthropy, but they focus on political power, occult rituals, as well as secret partnerships and oaths within the brotherhood. 2 Corinthians 11:13-15 tells us that Satan himself masquerades as an angel of good will:

> For such people are false apostles, deceitful workers, masquerading as apostles of Christ. And no wonder, for Satan himself masquerades as an angel of light. It is not surprising, then, if his servants also masquerade as servants of righteousness. Their end will be what their actions deserve. (NIV)

And Mathew 5:34-37 forbids swearing oaths:

> But I tell you, do not swear an oath at all: either by heaven, for it is God's throne; or by the earth, for it is his footstool; or by Jerusalem, for it is the city of the Great King. And do not swear by your head, for you cannot make even one hair white or black. All you need to say is simply "Yes" or "No"; anything beyond this comes from the evil one. (NIV)

The god of Freemasonry is a universal God that shares his throne with all faiths. While they focus greatly on the Old Testament, they neglect Christ as the Way, the Truth, and the Light. The Mason searches from the light of wisdom, but neglects Jesus, the true Light of the world. John 8:12 says, "Then spake Jesus again unto them, saying, I am the light of the world: he that followeth me shall not walk in darkness, but shall have the light of life." (KJV)

Albert Pike, a leader in the Masons, states in his book *Morals and Dogma*:

> ... Masonry existed as it now exists, the same in spirit and at heart, before even the first colonies emigrated into Southern India, Persia, and Egypt, from the cradle of humans (ancient Babylon). "We reproduce the speculations of Philosophers, the Kabbalist, the My stagogues and the Gnostics."[15]

> Masons perceive a select few elite individuals have access to special knowledge passed on by the ancients, they carry the torch as the selected group. Relating to the ancients..."But their doctrines on this subject were esoteric; they did not communicate them to the people at large, but only to a favored few; and as they were communicated in Egypt and India, in Persia and Phenicia, in Greece and Samothrace, in the greater mysteries, to the Initiates. The communication of this knowledge and other secrets, some of which are perhaps lost, constituted, under other names, what we now call Masonry, or

---

15 *Morals And Dogma* (Illustrated): The Reader's Digital Edition, By Albert Pike.

Free or Frank-Masonry. That knowledge was, in one sense, the Lost Word, which was made known to the Grand Elect, Perfect, and Sublime Masons."[16]

Masons trace their roots to ancient Babylon and ancient Egypt. Considering America's Masonic heritage, we can assume, many of the monuments in Washington, DC, pay homage to ancient Egyptian gods. The Washington Monument, built to commemorate George Washington, is the exact shape of an obelisk relating to the Egyptian god Osiris. The obelisk faces the Jefferson Memorial, a dome-shaped structure that represents the Egyptian goddess, Isis. The monuments are aligned to represent the marriage of these two Egyptian gods, the male penis of the god Osiris and the womb of Isis. It is even speculated that the number thirteen, relating to the first thirteen colonies, is a high masonic number connecting to the god Osiris. The number thirteen is duplicated on the great seal, numbering the levels of the pyramid.

In 1880, the Masons transported a 3,500-year-old obelisk representing a cornerstone of man's great achievements, which the Masons sought to build upon, across the sea to a key place in central park. Once it arrived, 9,000 Masons in full regalia accompanied its ceremonial placement.

The caption on the obelisk reads, "On October 9, 1880, the corner stone of the foundation for the Egyptian Obelisk was laid in Central Park under Grand Lodge auspices, with MW Jesse B. Anthony, *Grand Master*, in charge, and RW Edward ML Ehlers as Marshal of the Day."[17] Some say

---

16 Ibid.

17 *The New York Masonic Outlook*, The Board of General Activities of the Grand Lodge of New York, Boonville, January 1930, Vol. VI, No. 5.

the alignment of two other obelisks installed by the Masons mirror Orion's belt, similar to the pyramids of Giza.

During Grand Master Jesse B. Anthony's address, he said, "That [obelisk, for] which we have today laid the foundation stone, was one of two originally located at Heliopolis some 3,400 years ago, and afterwards, [1,903 years ago], removed to Alexandria, where they received the name of Cleopatra's Needles.[18]

This ancient Egyptian obelisk was a memorial stone and a worship monument to the Pharaoh of Egypt and the god Ra. Men associated with the Masons hoped to reach greater grandeur and illumination than their ancient brothers. Just as in the days of Babel, man sought to become like God, immortalized and worshipped, through feats of engineering. Those who want to follow the path of Babylon will surely arrive at the same fate.

Ephesians 2:19-22 proclaims our chief cornerstone as Jesus Christ, in whom we as Christians are planted on a firm foundation that cannot be moved:

> Consequently, you are no longer foreigners and strangers, but fellow citizens with God's people and members of his household, built on the foundation of the apostles and prophets, with Christ Jesus himself as the chief cornerstone. In him the whole building is joined together and rises to become a holy temple in the Lord. And in him you too are being built together to become a dwelling in which God lives by his Spirit. (NIV)

18 "Painting by Paul Orban, 1930, Obelisk Cornerstone Ceremony," by the Grand Lodge of Free and Accepted Masons of the State of New York, Mar 14, 2019. https://nymasons.org/site/painting-by-paul-orban-1930-obelisk-cornerstone-ceremony/

Although many in the order may subscribe to Christian faith in theory, the masonic faith aligns more with a New Age ideology that positions mankind to become gods of this world through great feats of achievement. This is reflected as far back as 1881:

> ... There is nothing done in masonry that is not for a purpose and is not designed to impress its lessons upon us. Let it be our endeavour therefore to lay the foundation of our character on a broad, sure and deep foundation...as will bear the application of the plumb, square and level; let us...build upon that foundation a character which is above reproach...And, when finally we have completed our task; erected a monument of moral grandeur and symmetry; achieved something which is for the welfare and advancement of the human race; then in after years the coming generations will treasure your memory, imitate your example, point to your deeds, and draw inspiration from your life as one worthy of their veneration.[19]

One of the most prominent masonic brothers was Norman Vincent Peale, a protestant minister best known for his book titled *The Power of Positive Thinking*. He was also a thirty-third degree Mason and New Age teacher. Many Christians see Peale's books as focused more on prosperity and self-help than a life submitted to the Word of God. Their official magazine was titled *New Age* until 1990 when

---

19 *Transactions of the Grand Lodge of Free and Accepted Masons of the State of New York*, Thomas Holman, Printer, New York, 1881, pp. 108-125.

it was retitled *The Scottish Rite Journal,* likely due to the speculative term being used more frequently.

In his book, *En Route to Global Occupation,* Gary Kah explains that he interviewed several Masons, and those who were still members had a drastically different testimony than those who had left the order. He says:

> They were fiercely loyal to the lodge and told me that Freemasonry was nothing more than an international secret fraternity based on good works. Former Masons, on the other hand, offered views that could not have been more opposite from those of their counterparts. They told me that the organization was anti-Christ and that it was dangerous, particularly in its higher levels, citing the previous as their main reason for leaving, adding that it was Luciferically inspired.[20]

In my personal communication with an ex-Mason, a private business owner and born-again Christian, he explained that he left the Order because the esoteric rituals conflicted with his religious beliefs. He explained that while many of the rituals required to move from a lower to a higher degree included biblical and ancient Egyptian symbolism, they are repurposed in an obscure way. He considered it blasphemous to use sacred biblical symbolism out of its direct context and meaning. He also disclosed that many men involved in the group had only a distant association with Christianity and that very few read the Bible on a consistent basis. He also said that Anglo-American and Afro-American Masons

---

20 *En Route to Global Occupation,* Gary Kah, Huntington House Publisher Copyright 1992, p. 107.

do not share a common lodge space in the Pennsylvania Lodge, and he felt this was unexpected in this current age.

Most men who are Masons joined the Order to experience kinship and favoritism centered on worldly alliances that build their influence or business. Men are usually introduced to the Order by a fellow Mason, and the deep esoteric truths of the secret societies are not disclosed at the beginning. Participants swear through threat of death that they will not willingly disclose information about the lodge to outsiders. But Leviticus 20:6 says, "'I will set my face against anyone who turns to mediums and spiritisms to prostitute themselves by following them, and I will cut them off from their people." (NIV)

America has deep Christian roots as well as deep occultic traditions that are evident in every realm of society. We are in a time when many mysteries are being disclosed and we can no longer be blind to this truth. We can exalt the true and living God or the God of the world. The choice is ours.

Chapter 9
1984

During the Obama administration, I was on a business trip in Paris, France, and I picked up an American quarter from the ground. Since I had found the American quarter in a foreign country, I asked that Lord, "What does this mean?" I had learned to discern the Lord's voice through signs and symbols, not taking these small encounters for granted.

The Holy Spirit prompted me to look at the date—1984. That date didn't have much relevance for me, so I Googled it, and the first thing that came to my attention was George Orwell's book, *1984: The Rise of Big Brother.* The Holy Spirit said, "This is what is happening in your government at this very moment."

In his book, Orwell warns us of the dangers of totalitarian government and the extent that government will go to keep power. All forms of government have the potential to enlarge unless closely regulated by a freedom-loving population.

Orwell also warns of the use of propaganda to control a deceived population. Not only can media be censored, but through alliances with technology companies, people can perceive they are searching for truth, but the search engines highlight the viewpoint of the company, creating an altered selection of articles. We are in a time of great deception that has never been experienced on such a global scale.

The Holy Spirit is the Spirit of truth, and He will lead us into all truth. This is our hope! The Lord also reveals hidden things. Daniel 2:22 says, "He reveals deep and hidden things; he knows what lies in darkness, and light dwells with him." (NIV) The kings of the earth can plot against Him and against the people, but the Lord will bring everything to light. We must trust in the counsel of the Holy Spirit to lead us and teach us.

A key theme of *1984* is the use of "newspeak," a term that describes the government's use of words to control the thoughts of the public. Newspeak is quite evident today. The positive terms are given to public polices with strong, negative outcomes.

Newspeak was also evident in the Ministry of Truth, whose purpose is to rewrite history to change the facts to fit party doctrine for propaganda effect. It's also evident in the Ministry of Love, referred to as "Miniluv," who is responsible for torture and fear tactics. Anyone who acts against Big Brother or the party, like Winston does in the novel, is tortured into submitting to the totalitarian government.

The Ministry of Plenty controlled the rations of the population. The fictitious society in Orwell's book operates within a rationing system, so it's not the generous agency that the name suggests. Rather, this ministry keeps members of society poor and in a perpetual state of wanting so that they are easier for Big Brother to control.

As a sort of political prophet, Orwell speaks from of the grave of what would be the result of absolute power and control over the people. According to an article in *Newsweek,* as of April 2022, the Biden administration implemented a disinformation campaign that many are comparing to the Ministry of Truth in *1984.*[21] Following is a quote from the article:

> On Wednesday, Homeland Security Secretary Alejandro Mayorkas testified during a budget hearing of the House Appropriations Subcommittee on Homeland Security that a Disinformation Governance Board had recently been created to fight the spread of disinformation on the internet.

Under the Biden administration, *1984* is becoming our new reality. The pandemic gave central government more power to enact control over information flow, and the American people were willing to give up many of their beloved freedoms under the guise of safety. The result is our freedom of information is slipping away under dystopian policies. Only time will tell if we can turn back the trends in favor of free speech and freedom.

The pandemic has given more ground to the alliance between global government, The Who, big tech, and multinational companies. These entities are coming together to push a global agenda and shut down

---

21 "Joe Biden's Disinformation Board Likened to Orwell's 'Ministry of Truth'," by Jon Jackson, *Newsweek* article, April 29, 2022. https://www. newsweek.com/joe-bidens-disinformation-board-likened-orwells-ministry-truth-1702190

individual thought. The horrors of Big Brother controlling the world are more credible today than ever before.

But this is nothing new under the sun. Ecclesiastes 1:9 says, "The thing that hath been, it is that which shall be; and that which is done is that which shall be done: and there is no new thing under the sun." (KJV) Man's quest for power has always been and will always be until the end of the age. Freedom as we have experienced it in America is a rare gift from God to those who have labored under the will of God. God has given mankind free will, and the devil and his global minions have tried to limit man's ability to choose.

The struggle for freedom has been ongoing throughout the generations. The difference today is that our advancements in technology can make global control a possibility. We only need to look to China and see how the Communist government is tracking their citizens with high-tech cameras and monitoring them on a social credit system.

The Holy Spirit recently provoked me to look at the 2022 quarter being distributed under the Biden administration. It has the image of Maya Angelou on one side, extended like an eagle, and a large image of George Washington on the other side. But George Washington's face is flipped in a new direction and is much larger than the previous quarter. I believe this is a sign that under the Biden Administration the nation is going in a new direction that includes a larger central government. The new direction of Washington's face is now facing away from the moto, "In God We Trust," Washington is effectively turning his back toward God, further asserting the current administration's stance toward the significance of "God" in

America. Much time and thought goes into the creation of a new coin, every detail has significant consideration around the design concept.

The Biden administration is quickly pushing us toward global government alliances. The Green New Deal is another high-budget project that links arms with the global community at the cost of high taxes and freedoms.

Chapter 10
Signs of a Nation
Under Judgment

Romans 1:18-32 says:

> The wrath of God is being revealed...against all...who suppress the truth... For since the creation of the world God's invisible qualities...have been clearly seen, being understood from what has been made, so that people are without excuse... although they knew God, they neither glorified Him as God nor gave thanks to Him... They exchanged the truth about God for a lie, and worshiped and served created things rather than the Creator... Because of this, God gave them over to shameful lusts... Furthermore, just as they did not think it worthwhile to retain the knowledge of God, so God gave them over to a depraved mind, so that they do what ought not to be done... they not only continue to do these very things but also approve of those who practice them. (NIV)

So what does a nation look like when it has been given up to people who have depraved minds? According to Romans 1:29-31, it is filled with unrighteousness, wickedness, and greed. Further, it is filled with envy, murder, strife, deceit, and malice. The people are gossips, slanderers, God-haters, insolent, arrogant and boastful. They invent ways of doing evil and are disobedient to their parents. They are senseless, faithless, heartless, and merciless. That sounds a lot like the America we see on the daily news. We are getting dangerously close to the climax of God's passive wrath on the United States.

Isaiah prophesied to Israel during a time of God's impending judgment. We can take note of the judgments that came upon the land of Israel and see how they relate to our current national condition.

Isaiah 3:4 says a sign of God's judgment is the youth of a nation ruling over them: "I will make mere youths their officials; children will rule over them." (NIV) Youth commonly don't have the experiential knowledge of history that their elders have. A country run by its youth is bound to fall into mistakes of the past. We see this happening today in America.

Young people are falling for the promises of socialism and communism that have destroyed the freedoms and prosperity of nations around the world. Youthful politicians like AOC, Alexandria Ocasio-Cortez, are winning congressional districts even though they have little experience. They are pushing the promises of socialism, free education, free housing, and the over-abundant spending that will send our nation into collapse. They are making abundant promises to the voting constituents with little ability to meet the needs of the nation's budget deficit.

History shows the promises of socialism commonly lead to catastrophe. In 1932-1933 socialists took privately owned farms and forced them into collective farming communities, which led to a mass famine that killed 3.9 million Ukrainians. Farmers were forced to abandon their land, and poor government management of resources left the Ukrainian population starving. The famine is known as Holodomor (the Terror-Famine or the Great Famine). Some recognize the Holodomor as genocide against the Ukrainian people.

This same type of famine resulted in the socialist revolution in China. Farm owners were lined up and shot, and the new socialist government redistributed their land to government-run farm collectives. Nearly 60 million people were killed in the great Chinese famine under Mao's new socialist government from 1958-1962. The lack of wisdom from youth running a nation's government results in history repeating itself.

Another sign of a nation under judgment is captivity. Israel had many seasons of freedom and captivity. The prophet Jeremiah warned Israel of the coming captivity under Babylonian rule. This was a judgment God brought upon the nation of Israel.

Captivity can come in many forms, in our modern era most captivity has come in the form of oppressive laws and restrictive forms of government. Covid-19 restrictions brought a new form of captivity and government control never experienced in America. Governors were given emergency powers that extended open-endedly closing private business and leading to a loss in livelihood and years of investment. Mandatory vaccines brought additional loss of body autonomy and loss of jobs. Although temporary in nature, a new level of power was given to state and federal government during the pandemic. The American people are now at the mercy of the World Health Organization and government officials to allow for basic freedoms.

Several local judges have since ruled against an obsessive use of power and select people that have lost their jobs have since returned to work. A recent ruling in a New York Supreme court on October 25, 2022, stated that all employees that were fired for being unvaccinated must be reinstated with back pay. The courts ruled, "being vaccinated does not prevent an individual from contracting or transmitting Covid-19." This ruling comprised 1,700 employees that were fired during the Covid-19 restrictions in New York City.[22]

Psalm 75:7 reveals that God sets up kings and he takes down kings. Even the wicked ruler can be ordained by the rule of God: "It is God who judges: He brings one down, he exalts another." (NIV)

Daniel 2:21 adds, "And He changeth the times and the seasons; He removeth kings and setteth up kings. He giveth wisdom unto the wise, and knowledge to them that know understanding." (KJV)

And finally, Jeremiah 25:4-12 says:

> And though the LORD has sent all his servants the prophets to you again and again, you have not listened or paid any attention. They said, "Turn now, each of you, from your evil ways and your evil practices, and you can stay in the land the LORD gave to you and your ancestors for ever and ever. Do not

22 https://www.foxnews.com/us/new-york-supreme-court-reinstates-all-employees-fired-being-unvaccinated-orders-backpay.amp?fbclid=IwAR0_hnQ-JRWIL5gL_iCPoe1wCM69oTs6l-Ku99MdEz2Dc5zhnM4P1k6O-foY

follow other gods to serve and worship them; do not arouse my anger with what your hands have made. Then I will not harm you."

"But you did not listen to me," declares the LORD, "and you have aroused my anger with what your hands have made, and you have brought harm to yourselves."

Therefore the LORD Almighty says this: "Because you have not listened to my words, I will summon all the peoples of the north and my servant Nebuchadnezzar king of Babylon," declares the LORD, "and I will bring them against this land and its inhabitants and against all the surrounding nations. I will completely destroy them and make them an object of horror and scorn, and an everlasting ruin. I will banish from them the sounds of joy and gladness, the voices of bride and bridegroom, the sound of millstones and the light of the lamp. This whole country will become a desolate wasteland, and these nations will serve the king of Babylon seventy years.

"But when the seventy years are fulfilled, I will punish the king of Babylon and his nation, the land of the Babylonians, for their guilt," declares the LORD, "and will make it desolate forever. (NIV)

Lack of sound Bible teaching can lead to judgment from God because it reveals that the nation's shepherds have turned away from Him. Judgment from God leads to an oppressive government and a decrease in freedoms.

Freedom to worship and freedom to work for an honest day's wages, on the other hand, are blessings from the Lord.

Ezekiel 34:1-4 says:

> The word of the Lord came to me: "Son of man, prophesy against the shepherds of Israel; prophesy and say to them: 'This is what the Sovereign Lord says: Woe to you shepherds of Israel who only take care of yourselves! Should not shepherds take care of the flock? You eat the curds, clothe yourselves with the wool and slaughter the choice animals, but you do not take care of the flock. You have not strengthened the weak or healed the sick or bound up the injured. You have not brought back the strays or searched for the lost. You have ruled them harshly and brutally. (NIV)

It is clear to most Christians that there has been a decrease of balanced teaching in the church. Sermons about prosperity, self-help, and good living outweighed sermons about the fear of the Lord, repentance, and true devotion to God.

Some American preachers arc being so bold as to preach death at the pulpit by advocating for abortion during their sermons. Pastor Jamal H. Bryant gave a pro-abortion speech at an Atlanta Megachurch, mockingly named, "New Birth." The pastor said the Supreme Court's decision to overturn Roe vs. Wade is part of "something satanic afoot in Washington, DC." This pointed sermon was given during baby dedications, which serve to anoint babies in the presence of the Lord.

How can a pastor representing the Author of Life stand firmly with the deaths of 60 million babies since

Roe vs. Wade was enacted? The hypocrisy is incredible, and it is a clear sign of the last days before the return of Christ. Has the gospel of Christ been diluted to the point that the church of God honors death over life?

This type of secularism has deceived a generation of young people into valuing their choices over preserving life, and only a restored heart can lead us to repentance. I pray that God restores the broken and deceived hearts of our nation.

I can hear the prophets of old twisting in their graves. How far have we fallen that this topic is even a point of contention in the Christian church?

Jeremiah 3:14-15 says, "'Return, faithless people,' declares the Lord, 'for I am your husband. I will choose you—one from a town and two from a clan—and bring you to Zion. Then I will give you shepherds after my own heart, who will lead you with knowledge and understanding.'" (NIV) At this point in history, Israel was in the midst of deep idolatry, and God was calling the people to return to Him. If the people's hearts returned to the Lord, He would give them shepherds after His own heart.

Isaiah 3:5 says, "People will oppress each other—man against man, neighbor against neighbor. The young will rise up against the old, the nobody against the honored." (NIV) Recent years have seen this scripture revealed clearly in the form of rioting due to accusations of racial injustice, neighbor against neighbor, and increased violence against the elderly in our metropolitan cities. The riots of the summer of 2020 resulted in burned-down businesses, looted stores, devasted cities, the great divide in American culture, and politics becoming even greater.

Isaiah 3:8-9 says, "Their words and deeds are against the Lord, defying his glorious presence. The look on their faces testifies against them; they parade their sin like Sodom; they do not hide it. Woe to them! They have brought disaster upon themselves." (NIV) Isaiah talks of a nation that flaunts its sin like a token on its chest. This is also evident when we speak of American society and culture. Abortion enthusiasts, for example, see little humanity in an unborn baby. In fact, American culture is some of the most desensitized to abortion. Consequently the sin of abortion is paraded as a woman's right to choose. In 2020, the state of New York passed new laws to allow for abortion up to birth.

Alternative sexual relationships are also postured as "normal." Explicit sexual activity is displayed on our TVs, in the music we listen to, and on social media. Now it's being pushed in our secular school curriculum. This type of content continues to escalate and be accepted as the new normal. Even our politicians are posting videos of sexual dances on social media platforms. A recent tweet from July 5, 2022, featured an elected Rhode Island State Senator, Tiara Mack, twerking on her head to promote her future election. The once-noble position of State Senator has now been downgraded to a freak show.

Isaiah 3:16 warned Israel that the celebration of lewd activity, a nation priding itself in sin and the worship of false gods, meant judgment upon the land: "The Lord says, 'The women of Zion are haughty, walking along with outstretched necks, flirting with their eyes, strutting along with swaying hips, with ornaments jingling on their ankles.'" (NIV)

Ezekiel 7:20-21 discusses a culture that continues to make idols of its possessions and serve them instead of the true and living God. Our marketplace is centered on worshipping the latest fashions, tech creations, beauty, fame, and wealth. This base desire to acquire and worship things is pushed on social media and in every commercial. The church and the culture alike have made an idol of wealth and possessions. Even our pastors are wearing Prada, Fendi, Gucci, and other overprice brands. Ezekiel warned the Israelites that God was not happy with this type of idolatry and that sudden judgment was upon them.

While we are not called to shun wealth, because God wants us to be prosperous, it is the love of money that corrupts a devoted heart. 1 Timothy 6:10 says, "For the love of money is a root of all kinds of evil. Some people, eager for money, have wandered from the faith and pierced themselves with many griefs." (NIV)

Ezekiel 7:20-21 also warned Israel that their wealth would be the plunder of foreigners: "They took pride in their beautiful jewelry and used it to make their detestable idols. They made it into vile images; therefore I will make it a thing unclean for them. I will give their wealth as plunder to foreigners and as loot to the wicked of the earth, who will defile it." (NIV)

America has been the most prosperous nation during the twenty-first century, but we see the winds of change blowing. As our GDP decreases, nations like China and India continue to increase and expand. Many of our jobs have been shipped overseas, leaving Americans unemployed and destitute. Since 1975 we have seen an overall decline in our manufacturing, leaving cities across the United States empty and without a future resource. Prosperous cities like Flint, Michigan, were nearly deserted in the 1980's when the car factories were closed, and car production was shipped overseas.

Ezekiel 7:27 says that God judges a nation according to its own conduct and by its own standards. That's how America will be judged: "The king will mourn, the prince will be clothed with despair, and the hands of the people of the land will tremble. I will deal with them according to their conduct, and by their own standards I will judge them. Then they will know that I am the Lord." (NIV)

Our God is rich in His mercy, but there comes a time when He will judge idolatry, the shedding of innocent blood, oppressing the poor, and leading innocent children astray. I believe we have reached the hour of judgment upon our land. I pray we wholeheartedly repent and turn our hearts back to the Lord.

Chapter 11
God's Appointed Time!

Scripture reveals that God has appointed times and seasons. The Old Testament is filled with appointed times and festivals. Leviticus 23:1-8 says:

> The Lord said to Moses, "Speak to the Israelites and say to them: 'These are my appointed festivals, the appointed festivals of the Lord, which you are to proclaim as sacred assemblies. These are the Lord's appointed festivals, the sacred assemblies you are to proclaim at their appointed times: The Lord's Passover begins at twilight on the fourteenth day of the first month. On the fifteenth day of that month the Lord's Festival of Unleavened Bread begins; for seven days you must eat bread made without yeast. On the first day hold a sacred assembly and do no regular work. For seven days present a food offering to the Lord. And on the seventh day hold a sacred assembly and do no regular work.'" (NIV)

Psalm 102:13 and Psalm 75 reveal that God has an appointed time for favor and an appointed time for judgment. Psalm 102:13 says, "You will arise *and* have mercy on Zion; For the time to favor her, Yes, the set time, has come." (NKJV)

And Psalm 75 says:

> We praise you, God, we praise you, for your Name is near; people tell of your wonderful deeds.
>
> You say, "I choose the appointed time; it is I who judge with equity. When the earth and all its people quake, it is I who hold its pillars firm. To the arrogant I say, 'Boast no more,' and to the wicked, 'Do not lift up your horns. Do not lift your horns against heaven; do not speak so defiantly.'"
>
> No one from the east or the west or from the desert can exalt themselves. It is God who judges: He brings one down, he exalts another. In the hand of the Lord is a cup full of foaming wine mixed with spices; he pours it out, and all the wicked of the earth drink it down to its very dregs.
>
> As for me, I will declare this forever; I will sing praise to the God of Jacob, who says, "I will cut off the horns of all the wicked, but the horns of the righteous will be lifted up." (NIV)

The Israelites have witnessed times of lack (their desert wanderings), captivity, and restoration. God ordained all these seasons and always provided for them.

Daniel 11:27 reveals there is also an appointed time of the end: "The two kings, with their hearts bent on evil, will sit at the same table and lie to each other, but to no avail, because an end will still come at the appointed time." (NIV)

1 Corinthians 4:5 warns not to judge anything before the appointed time: "Therefore, judge nothing before the appointed time; wait until the Lord comes. He will bring to light what is hidden in darkness and will expose the motives of the heart. At that time each will receive their praise from God." (NIV)

The time of the end is the Second Coming of Christ, a time of God's righteous judgment, a time of great tribulation like we have never seen before. When Jesus was asked about the end of the age and His Second Coming, He revealed in Matthew 24:3-8:

> Tell us they said, "when will this happen, and what will be the sign of your coming and of the end of the age?"

> Jesus answered: "Watch out that no one deceives you. For many will come in my name, claiming, 'I am the Messiah,' and will deceive many. You will hear of wars and rumors of wars but see to it that you are not alarmed. Such things must happen, but the end is still to come. Nation will rise against nation, and kingdom against kingdom. There will be famines and earthquakes in various places. All these are the beginning of birth pains. (NIV)

Ecclesiastes 3:3-8 discusses a time and season for everything:

There is a time for everything, and a season for every activity under the heavens: a time to be born and a time to die, a time to plant and a time to uproot, a time to kill and a time to heal, a time to tear down and a time to build, a time to weep and a time to laugh, a time to mourn and a time to dance, a time to scatter stones and a time to gather them, a time to embrace and a time to refrain from embracing, a time to search and a time to give up, a time to keep and a time to throw away, a time to tear and a time to mend, a time to be silent and a time to speak, a time to love and a time to hate, a time for war and a time for peace. (NIV)

The time when God will come and bring unity to all things in heaven and on earth is quickly approaching. Ephesians 1:8-10 says, "With all wisdom and understanding, he made known to us the mystery of his will according to his good pleasure, which he purposed in Christ, to be put into effect when the times reach their fulfillment—to bring unity to all things in heaven and on earth under Christ." (NIV)

As believers we await this time of God's perfect unity, when all things will be brought under the authority of Christ. Revelation 20:1-3 reveals that at this time Satan will be bound for 1,000 years and the righteous will rejoice:

And I saw an angel coming down out of heaven, having the key to the Abyss and holding in his hand a great chain. He seized the dragon, that ancient serpent, who is the devil, or Satan, and bound him for a thousand years. He threw him into the Abyss, and locked and sealed it over him, to keep him from deceiving the nations anymore until the thousand years were ended. After that, he must be set free for a short time. (NKJV)

One of the most shocking transitions in American culture has been the sexualizing of the youth. Targeting the children with perverted sexually explicit activity is a telling sign that the forces at work in our nation are fundamentally evil and we are approaching the "Days of Noah" prophesied by Jesus Christ. Much of this sexualization is currently coming in the form of queer education and entertainment. Organizations have been formed in recent years to bring queer entertainers to perform for young children and have been welcome as entertainment and mentors in churches.

A quest for sexual freedom should not center on exposing the youth to depraved sexual behavior. We tell our children that this type of activity advocates freedom and happiness without any regard for God's Word. Drag queens preach in our churches as a sign of sexual liberty. Targeting the children with perverted sexually explicit activity is a telling sign that the forces at work in our nation are fundamentally evil.

An organization called, "Drag Queen Story hour" has a focus on teaching young children to embrace queer lifestyles by exposing youth to drag queens. The organization hosts events in bookstores, schools, and libraries. They say on their website, "DQSH captures the imagination and play of the gender fluidity of childhood and gives kids glamorous, positive, and unabashedly queer role models."[23]

---

23 "What is drag story hour?" https://www.dragstoryhour.org/about

The femistcurrent.com expounds, "Drag queens and drag culture tend to be hypersexualized, mimicking strippers in revealing costumes; portraying exaggerated, objectified 'women' performing sexualized dances; and using explicit language throughout. Needless to say, drag is inappropriate for children."[24]

Jesus has a special love for our children, and Matthew 18:6 warns of the punishment that awaits those who lead them astray: "If anyone causes one of these little ones—those who believe in me—to stumble, it would be better for them to have a large millstone hung around their neck and to be drowned in the depths of the sea." (NIV)

It saddens me that we are in such a lost generation that the Prophet Nahum would be stunned. I personally do not stand in judgment on anyone seeking alternative lifestyles, but God will judge all of us according to our own deeds and His righteousness.

In countless ways we are a nation that has turned our back on the ways of God. God is mocked in our movies, and on many popular talk shows, "Jesus Christ" is often heard as a curse word in popular films. A broad portion of Americans entertain themselves with violence, witchcraft, and lust, and our disgrace is ever present before a holy and perfect Creator. Before the judgment of Noah's day, Genesis 6:5-6 says that wickedness had greatly increased on the Earth:

> The Lord saw how great the wickedness of the human race had become on the earth, and that every

---

24 "Why do our children need "Drag Queen Story Hour?" by Alline Cormier, https://www.feministcurrent.com/2022/06/26/why-do-children-need-drag-queen-story-hour/

inclination of the thoughts of the human heart was only evil all the time. The Lord regretted that he had made human beings on the earth, and his heart was deeply troubled. (NIV)

Jesus said that as in the days of Noah, so will it be when He returns to Earth. We are fast approaching that hour. Revelation 18:2 says:

> With a mighty voice he shouted: "Fallen! Fallen is Babylon the Great!" She has become a dwelling for demons and a haunt for every impure spirit, a haunt for every unclean bird, a haunt for every unclean and detestable animal. (NIV)

America has become a haunt for every unclean spirit and detestable practice. We have fallen gravely short of founder Puritan John Winthrop's expectation as a "City on the Hill," a community of people that would be the salt and light of the world, inspired by Jesus's Sermon on the Mount.

A 100-year-old, World War II Marine Corps veteran, Carl Spurlin Dekel, recently said that this is not the America he fought to preserve and that he is deeply worried about America's future. "People don't realize what they have," he said. "The things we did and the things we fought for and the boys that died for it, it's all gone down the drain."[25] Our nation has

---

25 100-Year-Old WW2 Veteran Breaks Down: "This Is Not The Country We Fought For," posted by RCP Video on July 4, 2022. https://www.realclear-politics.com/video/2022/07/04/100-year-old_veteran_breaks down_this_is_not_the_country_we_fought_for.html

reached a point defamation, from which we will never return without the mercy of the Almighty God. Proverbs 14:34 says, "Righteousness exalts a nation, but sin condemns any people."

God has a great desire for all mankind to receive His mercy over His judgment, but mercy follows repentance. We must first turn from our sins and receive God's gift of eternal salvation through Jesus Christ our Lord. This may not change the judgments coming upon the land, but it will change our individual standing in front of a holy and perfect Creator.

Chapter 12
God's Righteous Judgment

As I continued to rely on the Lord as I wrote this book, He revealed that the word *judgment* has been changed to *justice* in most translations. As I was reading an older copy of the Bible in the original King James Version and comparing it with the New King James Version, I noticed in Isaiah 30:18 that "the God of Judgment" in the KJV had been changed to "the God of Justice" in the NKJV.

The KJV says, "And therefore will the Lord wait, that he may be gracious unto you, and therefore will he be exalted, that he may have mercy upon you: for the Lord is a God of **judgment**: blessed are all they that wait for him." (emphasis mine)

The NKJV says, "Therefore the Lord will wait, that He may be gracious to you; And therefore He will be exalted, that He may have mercy on you. For the Lord *is* a God of **Justice**; Blessed *are* all those who wait for Him." (emphasis mine)

Although *judgment* and *justice* can be interchangeable, I wonder if political correctness has impacted many modern versions of the Bible. Are we opposed to God's righteous judgment? Does God not have the right to judge His own creation? God, in His mercy, gave us a way to escape His righteous judgment in the person and sacrifice of Jesus Christ. Those who receive His salvation are no longer subject to judgment but to mercy.

Isaiah 30:1-3 highlights a time when Israel was trusting more in the strength of Egypt to come to their aid than trusting in God:

> Woe to the rebellious children, saith the Lord, that take counsel, but not of me; and that cover with a covering, but not of my spirit, that they may add sin to sin: That walk to go down into Egypt and have not asked at my mouth; to strengthen themselves in the strength of Pharaoh, and to trust in the shadow of Egypt! Therefore shall the strength of Pharaoh be your shame, and the trust in the shadow of Egypt your confusion. (KJV)

This is a common flaw of mankind, continuing to cling to the advancements of man and the power of our military to lead our nation instead of trusting in the power of God. Israel was trusting in foreign alliances.

Trusting in man over God leads to unnecessary oppression and crookedness. We see these attributes so present in our current political climate. More and more people are trusting in historically oppressive forms of government control like socialism and communism as solutions to national problems. A nation that puts their trust in manmade alliances over God is sure to fail, especially a nation that has a covenant with the living God.

Isaiah 30:12-13 warns of a sudden destruction coming on the nation of Israel. The aid of man's support is like a tall wall that is easily broken: "Wherefore thus saith the Holy One of Israel, because ye despise this word, and trust in oppression and perverseness, and stay thereon: Therefore this iniquity shall be to you as a breach ready to fall, swelling out in a high wall, whose breaking cometh suddenly at an instant." (KJV)

Isaiah 31:3 adds, "Now the Egyptians are men, and not God; and their horses flesh, and not spirit. When the Lord shall stretch out his hand, both he that helpeth shall fall, and he that is holpen shall fall down, and they all shall fail together." (KJV)

I see Isaiah's prophecies as warnings to all nations that trust in man over God.

Deuteronomy 32:4 says that God is perfect and His judgment is an aspect of His perfection: "He is the Rock, his work is perfect: for all his ways are judgment: a God of truth and without iniquity, just and right is he." (KJV)

In the book of Exodus, God brought the Israelites out of slavery by mighty acts of judgment upon the land of Egypt. These judgments moved Pharaoh's heart to eventually release millions of Israelite slaves. Exodus 6:6 says, "Therefore, say to the Israelites: "I am the Lord, and I will bring you out from under the yoke of the Egyptians. I will free you from being slaves to them, and I will redeem you with an outstretched arm and with mighty acts of judgment." (NIV)

Exodus 12:12 says that this judgment the Lord was bringing upon Egypt was a judgment upon the heads of their false gods: "On that same night I will pass through Egypt and strike down every firstborn of both people and animals, and I will bring judgment on all the gods of Egypt. I am the Lord." (NIV)

God judges with complete and perfect equity. Therefore, we can cast our trials upon the Lord and stand content that His judgment is just. Note Psalm 9:7-10:

> The Lord reigns forever; he has established his throne for judgment. He rules the world in righteousness and judges the peoples with equity. The Lord is a refuge for the oppressed, a stronghold in times of trouble. Those who know your name trust in you, for you, Lord, have never forsaken those who seek you. (NIV)

This world is full of generational conflicts, some continuing for more than a thousand years. These conflicts continue because the people seek revenge. God has an appointed time for all conflicts and wickedness on Earth to cease, a time for the restoration of all things, but first He will judge every person for his or her own iniquities. Some will go to everlasting bliss and others to everlasting damnation. God's mercy is captured in the full forgiveness of our sins by receiving His gift of salvation through the blood of Christ.

Chapter 13
The Six Woes

The prophet Isaiah highlights six woes, or six things that caused God great sadness and brought judgment upon Israel. Isaiah 5:7 recounts a man planting a vineyard that produces only bad fruit. When the landowner looked upon his vineyard, he was greatly distressed, so he proclaims he will uproot the vineyard and destroy it: "And he looked for justice, but saw bloodshed; for righteousness, but heard cries of distress." (NIV)

Next, the message of the six woes begins, starting with the first woe in Isaiah 5:8: "Woe to you who add house to house and join field to field till no space is left and you live alone in the land." (NIV) Isaiah is proclaiming that cultivating all the land and not leaving any for the poor can bring upon judgment. This message also relates to Haggai 1 when the Israelites were busy building their paneled houses while the Lord's house lay in ruins.

Isaiah 5:9-10 pronounces the judgment on Israel for this sin: "Surely the great houses will become desolate, the fine mansions left without occupants. A ten-acre vineyard will produce only a bath of wine; a homer of seed will yield only an ephah of grain." (NIV)

When we listen to these verses, we can see our modern cities and suburban communities full of people captured by their daily lives. Most of the people were more concerned with building their elaborate mansions than following the will of God. This may seem innocent at first glance, but God had set these people apart to be a holy priesthood, an example for the neighboring nations, and they were expected to live lives worthy of the God they worshipped.

The church of Jesus Christ is also called to be a holy priesthood, separated to further the purpose of God on Earth. Unfortunately, I see much of the modern church captured by the ways of the world, with little to distinguish the church from unbelievers. The message of walking in holiness, dying to self, and living to fulfil the Lord's Great Commission is often overlooked for a more pleasing message of encouragement and prosperity. Are we building our own mansions or our we building God's kingdom? Each of us must reflect on our own lives and discern for ourselves.

Isaiah 5:11-12 spells out the second woe on Israel: "Woe to those who rise early in the morning to run after their drinks, who stay up late at night till they are inflamed with wine. They have harps and lyres at their banquets, pipes and timbrels and wine, but they have no regard for the deeds of the Lord, no respect for the work of his hands." (NIV)

Isaiah is declaring that these people are more interested in running after pleasure and parties than after the things of God. They are a far cry from the priestly nation that God intended. Social functions and holidays have taken precedence over the commands of God. While the pleasure of parties is not out of line in total, the constant practice of revelry as a lifestyle can bring a rebuke from the Lord.

Isaiah 5:13-15 pronounces the judgment for this sin:

> Therefore my people will go into exile for lack of understanding; those of high rank will die of hunger and the common people will be parched with thirst. Therefore Death expands its jaws, opening wide its mouth; into it will descend their nobles and masses with all their brawlers and revelers. So people will be brought low and everyone humbled, the eyes of the arrogant humbled. (NIV)

Isaiah 5:18-19 discusses the third woe upon the nation of Israel: "Woe to those who draw sin along with cords of deceit, and wickedness as with cart ropes, to those who say, 'Let God hurry; let him hasten his work so we may see it. The plan of the Holy One of Israel—let it approach, let it come into view, so we may know it.'" (NIV)

Isaiah is describing someone is so actively engaged in their sin that they pull it in with ropes, welcome it, and hope to ensnare others in it. They carry their wickedness in carts so they can more easily distribute it among the nation. The people have become arrogant, rushing the things of God, asking for proof of what has been spoken by the prophets.

This same pride exists today. Many people will say, "I'll believe it when I see it." This is even common in church circles. Many churches are aligning more with the ways of the world than with the ways of God.

The fourth woe is in Isaiah 5:20: "Woe to those who call evil good and good evil, who put darkness for light and light for darkness, who put bitter for sweet and sweet for bitter." (NIV) This woe is describing a people who are so deep in their sin that the righteous are persecuted for aligning with the commands and ways of God, and the wicked are exalted as righteous. Darkness is marketed as light and evil is elevated as morally good.

We have reached this very point in our culture. Sexual perversion is welcomely promoted in our society, bloodshed is labeled as a woman's right to choose, and many churches teach love of self and love of money over servanthood. This fourth woe is the true measure of guilt upon a nation.

The fifth woe upon the nation of Israel is in Isaiah 5:21: "Woe to those who are wise in their own eyes and clever in their own sight." (NIV) This a nation that seeks after worldly wisdom instead of God. They even praise their own wisdom as if they are gods. They have reached the fullness of the tree of the Knowledge of Good and Evil and have become as gods. In the past, America has repented to seek wisdom and support from God. We still have a remanent that seeks God's wisdom on the land, but our current cultural norms better represent the whole of the nation.

The sixth woe on Israel is in Isaiah 5:22-23: "Woe to those who are heroes at drinking wine and champions at mixing drinks, who acquit the guilty for a bribe, but deny justice to the innocent." (NIV) This represents those who prefer to engage in revelry than to chase after the things of God. There is no difference between their practices and those of the unsaved. They have turned corrupt by chasing after their own desires, are easily tempted by bribery, and have little regard for justice and the innocent. This is a culture of people consumed with self.

The seventh woe is mentioned in Isaiah 31:1: "Woe to those who go down to Egypt for help, who rely on horses, who trust in the multitude of their chariots and in the great strength of their horsemen, but do not look to the Holy One of Israel, or seek help from the LORD." (NIV)

It's common for mankind to look toward worldly alliances for support during times of hardship. This message is a clear warning that we cannot trust in the strength of those alliances or our own strength as a nation. We must redirect our trust and hope in God's supernatural provision.

Difficult times are upon us now in the aftermath of COVID-19 with overwhelming government spending and debt. The outlook for continued prosperity in America is grim. Our hope is redirecting our attention from government to God.

Chapter 14
The Sword of God's Judgment Upon the Land

The word the Lord gave me was quake, meaning there will be a great shaking in our nation that will affect our land, finances, government, and everything we hold as a security blanket outside of God. This is just the beginning; more is to come. It's time to turn toward Jesus with all your heart, soul, and mind. Come under the wings of His shelter and trust in the Lord to preserve you during difficult times.

A great sword is coming to America. This will likely be war, and many will be displaced from their homes. God has also highlighted the city of New York as a target for attack. God's protection and provision over certain states will be evident as they align with godly principles and God's righteousness. States that are promoting and practicing abortion and other forms of corruption will be at great risk for disaster.

Isaiah 59:18 says, "According to their deeds, accordingly he will repay, fury to his adversaries, recompense to his enemies; to the islands he will repay recompense." (KJV)

The Lord is bringing to mind Ezekiel 9:4-6, which spells out the judgment that came upon Israel in Ezekiel's day:

> And the Lord said to him, "Go through the midst of the city, through the midst of Jerusalem, and set a mark upon the foreheads of the men who sigh and groan for all the abominations that are done in its midst." To the others He said in my hearing, "Go after him through the city and strike. Do not let your eye spare or have pity. Utterly slay old and young, both maidens and little children, and women. But do not touch any man on whom is the mark. And begin at My sanctuary." Then they began with the elders who were before the temple. (MEV)

We must feel remorse for the sins of our nation, which include idolatry, murder, ungodliness, sexual sin, and rebellion, and take no part in them. America and Israel have been blessed by God, and certain founders made public covenants with the God of the Bible.

God, in His mercy, has also given time for Israel and the United States to repent of their sin. Ezekiel 14:12-23, however, speaks of a time when there was no more time for repentance, and God brought four judgments upon Israel, and these judgments were final:

Jerusalem's Judgment Inescapable

> The word of the Lord came to me: "Son of man, if a country sins against me by being unfaithful and I stretch out my hand against it to cut off its food supply and send famine upon it and kill

its people and their animals, even if these three men—Noah, Daniel and Job—were in it, they could save only themselves by their righteousness, declares the Sovereign Lord.

"Or if I send wild beasts through that country and they leave it childless and it becomes desolate so that no one can pass through it because of the beasts, as surely as I live, declares the Sovereign Lord, even if these three men were in it, they could not save their own sons or daughters. They alone would be saved, but the land would be desolate.

"Or if I bring a sword against that country and say, 'Let the sword pass throughout the land,' and I kill its people and their animals, as surely as I live, declares the Sovereign Lord, even if these three men were in it, they could not save their own sons or daughters. They alone would be saved.

"Or if I send a plague into that land and pour out my wrath on it through bloodshed, killing its people and their animals, as surely as I live, declares the Sovereign Lord, even if Noah, Daniel and Job were in it, they could save neither son nor daughter. They would save only themselves by their righteousness.

"For this is what the Sovereign Lord says: How much worse will it be when I send against Jerusalem my four dreadful judgments—sword and famine and wild beasts and plague—to kill its men and their animals! Yet there will be some survivors—sons and daughters who will be brought out of it. They will come to you, and when you see their conduct and their actions, you will be consoled regarding the disaster I have brought on Jerusalem—every disaster I have brought on it. You will be consoled when you see their conduct and their actions, for you will know that I have done nothing in it without cause, declares the Sovereign Lord." (NIV)

Like Israel, America has also rebelled against God's ways and laws, bringing upon ourselves a similar judgment. We are in a time when deep darkness will begin to cover the Earth. This is sign that the Lord's return is near. As things get more chaotic, the Kingdom of Heaven is converging with the kingdom of this world. The blood of Jesus and true repentance, where we find God's grace and mercy, cover us from God's judgment. Look up because your redemption is near.

Chapter 15
Similarities Between America and Rome

There are many similarities between America and ancient Rome. Rome has influenced our Republican form of government, our architecture, and our liberal culture. While some of these influences have led to a free and vibrant society, the decadence and moral corruption of the Romans have contributed to America's downfall. Many people fear that if we don't change our ways and learn from the past we are doomed to repeat the same mistakes.

American founders modeled our form of government after the Roman Republic, creating executive and legislative branches of government, to balance power and prevent one party from ruling. Also like Rome, America created a system of written laws that citizens were required to follow. Both countries also have their own currency.

Rome had a long period of prosperity and little to no inflation when their currency was gold or silver. As they moved away from the gold standard they started

clipping their coins, which debased their money supply and resulted in inflation.

America has gone a similar route. Initially we had the
gold standard, which allowed for a true evaluation of our
currency. Under President Nixon in 1971, however, the
gold standard was removed, and the American dollar became a fiat currency, meaning it was no longer backed by
gold or silver, but by faith in the American government.

Fiat currency makes the American dollar much more vulnerable to inflation. In 2021 the Federal Reserve increased
the money supply by 40 percent in response to COVID stim-
ulus packages. The following year, the price of food went up
more than 10 percent, and prices continue to climb.

With the U.S. debt over 30 trillion, inflation is the biggest fear in today's vulnerable economy. When governments start increasing the money supply like we are experiencing today, prices go up. As a result, people living on
minimum wage are unable to buy the goods they need, and
increased public assistance is needed. Rome had public-as-
sistance programs called "Bread and Circus," which distributed food daily and provided free tickets to entertainment.

Bread and Circus was an incentive to keep the people of Rome happy during times of inflation. The
result, however, was government overspending and
more inflation. Today, we have politicians offering free
school, student debt removal, and free phones, the financial burden of which is passed on to the American
people. The result of increased government spending
is increased debt, instability, and inflation.

Because of Rome's growing economic problems, the
country was no longer able to financially support a large
army, and its borders weakened. As a result, hostile tribes

such as the Huns, Goths, and Vandals were able to enter Rome and pillage the city.

Although significantly less hostile overall, America is experiencing increased migration from Central and South America, which is putting a burden on social programs and taxpayers. An increase in taxes adds to increased political tension and overall dialogue. Weakened borders decrease the overall security of a nation.

Also, both Rome and America have a history of slavery. Rome had a large slave class that served their elite population of rulers. And while many people would like to forget the stain of slavery on American history, it has participated in shaping the culture and political discourse. Slavery in Roman times went beyond racial barriers and included all conquered territories. Over time, however, many slaves were able to purchase their freedom.

Both countries have also experienced a significant moral decline. Rome was founded on virtue and fidelity but later gave into slothfulness, selfish ambition, sexual depravity, lust for power, and debauchery. The great wealth and power of the Roman empire was falling to internal power struggles and moral decay.

Historian Will Durant says when speaking of the decline of Rome, "A great civilization is not conquered from without, until it has destroyed itself from within. The essential causes of Rome's decline lay in her people, her morals, her class struggle, her failing trade, her bureaucratic despotism, her stifling taxes, her consuming wars."[26]

---

26 Will Durant, Ariel Durant (1944). "The Story of Civilization: Caesar and Christ, a history of Roman civilization and of Christianity from their beginnings to A.D. 325."

Likewise, the American people once prided themselves on virtue and liberty but are now more focused on pushing moral boundaries; redefining family structure, sexual norms, and gender; and becoming more dependent on a government that is profiting on slander and lies.

Will America suffer the same fate as Rome? I foresee a decline that is unavoidable.

Chapter 16
A House Divided Cannot Stand

Because of our weakened state as a nation as a result of inner turmoil and political factions, our enemies have an opportunity to revolt against us. This news should be leading every Christian into significant prayer for God to intercede. Jesus says in Matthew 12:25, "Every kingdom divided against itself is brought to desolation; and every city or house divided against itself **shall not stand**." (KJV, emphasis mine)

King Solomon imposed heavy taxes during his reign to build the temple. After the temple was built, however, the people expected the tax to decrease. Unfortunately, Solomon's son, Rehoboam, who took the throne after King Solomon died, continued to aggressively tax the Israelites, which led to civil war. As a result, the nation of Israel separated into the Northern Kingdom (Israel) and the Southern Kingdom (Judah).

The Southern Kingdom had some righteous kings, like Asa, who attempted to remove the idolatry from the land and reestablish the laws of God. The Northern Kingdom, however, continued its move deeper into idolatry. Their most prominent king was Ahab and his wife, Jezebel, both of whom actively rebelled against the will and law of God. The Northern Kingdom was conquered by the Assyrians, leaving Judah the only remaining Kingdom standing. Over time, Judah was also led into idolatry and eventually Babylonian exile.

America is more divided than it has ever been, primarily due to a persistent spiritual battle of ideals. Some people want to take America into a New Age of global government and thought, sexual ambiguity, technocracy, and Earth worship. Others would like to restore America's foundation, built on individual freedoms, faith, moral tradition, and family. This deep divide is inherently spiritual and requires prayer and intercession.

Divisive language and manipulative media voices have stoked our nation's divide. Accusations of racism, hate, and fascism are pushed like candy to an American audience ripe for gossip. The people who seem to excel at the ugly game of American politics are those who are willing to punch their opponent the hardest.

The sad part of this unfortunate division is that many people on both sides of the political spectrum proclaim to follow Christ. This hate mongering has divided America and it has divided the American church. Jesus proclaims in Matthew 5:9, "Blessed are the peacemakers for they shall be called sons of God." (NKJV)

The Prince of Peace is looking down on His church and praying we will walk out the words He spoke. This starts with reestablishing the truth of God's Word and letting it take prominence in our lives. When the church decides to represent the Kingdom of God rather than the political storyline, we will see the love of God change the hearts of the people in our nation.

In the days of Nehemiah, the walls of Israel were in ruins. God sent Nehemiah, a man in the king's court, to rebuild the ruined wall. Today, the walls of our church are dilapidated, and we need peace makers to help restore relationships. Religious sects of Christianity have stood in our nation for centuries. While some of our doctrinal disputes are valid, others come from a spirit of division. Titus 3:9-11 warns the church about divisions based on the law:

> But avoid foolish controversies and genealogies and arguments and quarrels about the law, because these are unprofitable and useless. Warn a divisive person once, and then warn them a second time. After that, have nothing to do with them. You may be sure that such people are warped and sinful; they are self-condemned. (NIV)

God is repairing some of these breaches and bringing devoted followers of Christ into unity through His Spirit. We are one body in Christ, not under the law but under grace.

After the rebuilding the wall, Nehemiah appointed Ezra to read the law to bring unity under the true Word of God. As God's global church, we should have unity under God's holy Word. To have that unity, we need to reestablish the truths of the Word, remove the idolatry from among us, and stop conforming to cultural shifts. We need to put our trust in the God we proclaim and less in worldly riches and power. If our church is divided and callous, who will speak peace to this broken world?

I considered returning to politics, but one night God gave me a dream. I saw the political discourse, which looked like a bunch of kangaroos boxing in suits. God revealed that if I entered this discourse, I wouldn't contribute to a solution to the problem. I would just get punched repeatedly and end up punching back like a kangaroo, and it would all look like a giant boxing match. I decided I would rather preach the Gospel of reconciliation and be a voice for peace.

God will have the final say of what will happen in the nations of the world. With a renewed trust in His Word, we can have joy during trials. In Daniel 2:40-43, Nebuchadnezzar was given a dream about the coming Gentile kingdoms, with the fourth kingdom being divided:

> Finally, there will be a fourth kingdom, strong as iron—for iron breaks and smashes everything— and as iron breaks things to pieces, so it will crush and break all the others. Just as you saw that the feet and toes were partly of baked clay and partly of iron, so this will be a divided kingdom; yet it will have some of the strength of iron in it, even as you saw iron mixed with clay. As the toes were partly iron and partly clay, so this kingdom will be partly strong and partly brittle. And just as you saw the iron mixed with baked clay, so the people will be a mixture and will not remain united, any more than iron mixes with clay. (NIV)

Verses 44-45 contain the symbol of the rock, which is Christ, the rock of our salvation and the King of kings, who will set up His millennial Kingdom on Earth:

In the time of those kings, the God of heaven will set up a kingdom that will never be destroyed, nor will it be left to another people. It will crush all those kingdoms and bring them to an end, but it will itself endure forever. This is the meaning of the vision of the rock cut out of a mountain, but not by human hands—a rock that broke the iron, the bronze, the clay, the silver, and the gold to pieces. (NIV)

Chapter 17
Roe vs. Wade

While I was running for office, God told me that He would be overturning the mighty giant of Roe vs. Wade. That prophecy was fulfilled while I was writing this book. Many people have been praying tirelessly for this to happen for more than forty years. It's amazing to see God move in power! This generation of children being birthed in America will help bring our nation back to God.

In the days of Moses, a decree went out across Egypt to kill the male Israelite children. Moses was spared and he brought freedom to a nation. At the time of the Messiah's birth, King Herod issued a decree to kill all the boys in Bethlehem under age two in an attempt to kill the "King of the Jews." Matthew 2:16-18 says:

> When Herod realized that he had been outwitted by the Magi, he was furious, and he gave orders to kill all the boys in Bethlehem and its vicinity who were two years old and under, in accordance with the time he had learned from the Magi. Then what was

said through the prophet Jeremiah was fulfilled: "A voice is heard in Ramah, weeping and great mourning, Rachel weeping for her children and refusing to be comforted, because they are no more." (NIV)

While hundreds of babies were killed, Jesus was spared because an angel of the Lord warned Joseph of Herod's decree. Today, God wants to raise up a generation to usher in His Son's imminent return. The decree of death that has been a black cloud over America since 1973 will be removed over some states and present over others.

In Leviticus 20:2-5, God rebuked the Israelites for offering their children in the fire.

The Lord said to Moses, "Say to the Israelites: 'Any Israelite or any foreigner residing in Israel who sacrifices any of his children to Molek is to be put to death. The members of the community are to stone him. I myself will set my face against him and will cut him off from his people; for by sacrificing his children to Molek, he has defiled my sanctuary and profaned my holy name. If the members of the community close their eyes when that man sacrifices one of his children to Molek and if they fail to put him to death, I myself will set my face against him and his family and will cut them off from their people together with all who follow him in prostituting themselves to Molek.'" (NIV)

Although most people would not consider abortion as an offering to a pagan god, many have had abortions in the name of fulfilling financial dreams or self-preservation similar to those who worshipped Molek, a Canaanite god that required people to sacrifice their children. While Hollywood actress Michelle Williams was receiving a Golden Globe Award, she said, "I wouldn't have been able to do this without employing a woman's right to choose."[27]   How can anything sweet come out of such selfish ambition? James 3:16 warns, "For wherever there is jealousy and selfish ambition, there you will find disorder and evil of every kind." (NIV)

By the grace and mercy of God, we can change our minds at any time and ask for God's forgiveness. We have all fallen short and our understanding is limited.

Abortion is at the heart of God's righteous anger against America. Since 1970, our nation has authorized more than 60 million legal abortions. The number "60 million" is echoed in history's greatest atrocities, namely the 60 million people who were murdered under Stalin's communist regime in Russia and the 60 million who were murdered under Mao's communist transition in China.

Abortion deaths keep climbing by approximately 1 million American lives every year. The very act of legalizing abortion has positioned our nation to see abortion as a form of birth control. According to the Center for Disease Control, the annual number of legal induced abortions in the United States doubled between 1973 and 1979, and peaked in 1990.

In 2020 our nation glamorized abortion by running campaigns called "Shout Your Abortion" to encourage

---

27 Hollywood actress Michelle Williams credits abortion for her success in Golden Globes speech, *Blaze Media* article by Aaron Colen, January 6, 2020. https://www.theblaze.com/news/hollywood-actress-credits-success-to-ability-to-choose-abortion in golden-globes-speech

young women to be proud of having abortions. Social media campaigns have inspired young women to wear their abortion as a badge of honor.

I've never wanted to have children, so I had an abortion. I'm thriving, without guilt, without shame, without apologies. #ShoutYourAbortion

Our callous hearts have caused us to degrade the sanctity of life, resulting in increased sexual promiscuity and attacks on innocent blood. In the words of Judas Iscariot in Matthew 27:4, "'I have sinned,' he said, 'for I have betrayed innocent blood.'" (NIV)

Abortion is a multimillion-dollar business. Jude 1:11 warns, "What sorrow awaits them! For they follow in the footsteps of Cain, who killed his brother. Like Balaam, they deceive people for money. And like Korah, they perish in their rebellion." (NLT)

Abortions became common place during the Industrial Revolution. When men began working far from home, many would find the comforts of a prostitute. Prostitution became big business during the 19th century, and abortion accompanied the profession. Today, Planned Parenthood brings in nearly 1 billion a year in abortion revenue in the U.S. alone. The average cost of a first-term abortion is $400, and a second-trimester abortions can be upwards of $3,000.

A recent article on the Abort73 website said, "The abortion industry brings in approximately $831 million through their abortion services alone. If you add in the $337 million (or more) that Planned Parenthood (America's largest abortion provider) receives annually in government grants and contracts for, the annual dollar amount moves well past 1 billion."[28]

Politicians, media, and entertainment are all convincing young women to be sexually promiscuous in the name of putting themselves first and to choose abortion without regret. Our egocentric society exalts personal liberty without personal accountability for one's actions. With more liberty, an internal moral compass is necessary. As our culture shifts toward a secular, progressive worldview, we advocate for liberty, but we don't know what to do with it! As a result, our liberty has resulted in hedonism and decadence.

America the beautiful is dripping with the blood of the innocent. In New York City; New Jersey; and Washington, DC, 30 percent of all pregnancies were aborted in 2017. Genesis 4:10 states that Abel's blood cries out from the grave: "And the Lord said, 'What have you done? Listen; your brother's blood is crying out to me from the ground.'" (ESV) How much more of the blood of the innocent is crying out over America?

We have become a murderous nation, and the Lord has lifted His hand of justice against us! One of America's founding governors, John Winthrop, called America to be a city on the hill, shining the light of truth and righteousness to the nations. We have failed in this noble attempt to be a voice for justice.

---

28 "Abortions for profit," https://www.abort73.com/abortion/abortion_for_profit/

Jeremiah 22:3 shares the call of a righteous nation. It is the call to uphold justice and to protect the innocent: "Thus says the LORD: Do justice and righteousness and deliver from the hand of the oppressor him who has been robbed. And do no wrong or violence to the resident alien, the fatherless, and the widow, nor shed innocent blood in this place." (ESV)

Those without Christ can easily be swayed by the opinions of shifting change, and that is to be expected, but abortion divides the church as much as it divides the secular culture. Christians are called to be salt and light to a lost and dying world, but sadly the church is promoting the national agenda over the righteousness of God. The very act of aborting a baby is playing God; it is taking life and death into our own hands. We decide based on our own conscience who is worthy of life or death.

God reveals in Isaiah 55:8-9 that mankind has limited understanding, so we should not make such decisions. Instead, we should leave them up to God:

> "For my thoughts are not your thoughts, neither are your ways my ways," declares the Lord. "For as the heavens are higher than the earth, so are my ways higher than your ways and my thoughts than your thoughts." (ESV)

These words give me peace. I am happy that God's wisdom is exalted over my own. In my own lack of wisdom, I can come to God and ask for His wisdom and be guided through this eternal knowledge. Man's wisdom looks from a lens of lack, while God looks down from Heaven, a place of abundance. In God's unlimited abundance, He can provide everything we need if we ask Him to do so. Most babies are aborted due to financial insecurity and unstable relationships. Some of these difficult concerns can be solved if we learn to trust in God completely.

Lowering the abortion rates in America requires strong marriages and families, especially considering young women bear most of the difficult burden of raising a child. Men can play a key role in decreasing abortion by choosing to be husbands rather than just sexual partners.

My mother was a seventeen-year-old, minority, low-income, unmarried woman in 1975. There were times we didn't have a car or had to go without something we wanted, but as a whole God provided the necessities. Our true prosperity was having a relationship with the living God. My mother came to faith in her early twenties and passed the message of the gospel to her four children. We have all fallen short of following God completely, but His message and relationship has brought us unlimited guidance and prosperity. I declare to you today that God can provide in difficult situations, and He is a good, good Father. His Word is true and faithful.

Even after our children are born, they are continually invaded by spirits of lust, death, rage, and most recently identity, through the media and entertainment. We have allowed every unclean spirit to take up residence in our nation through all forms of entertainment and legislation.

I see no difference between our current culture and the whore of Babylon in Revelation 17 and 18. Revelation 18:2 says, "With a mighty voice he shouted: 'Fallen! Fallen is Babylon the Great!' She has become a dwelling for demons and a haunt for every impure spirit, a haunt for every unclean bird, a haunt for every unclean and detestable animal.'" (NIV)

As a society we have been negligent in protecting the innocent. We murder them in the womb due to inconvenience and we bombard them with entertainment that glorifies witchcraft, immorality, sexual perversion, and love of idols. This is a blatant attack from Satan himself and carried out by those that worship him.

Jesus said in Matthew 18:6, "But whoso shall offend one of these little ones which believe in me, it were better for him that a millstone were hanged about his neck, and that he were drowned in the depth of the sea." (KJV)

Our children are God's children, and He has given us stewardship over their hearts, minds, and souls. As a mother of three I know how difficult it is to protect them from all the filth in our society. But we need to protect them, both spiritually and physically. Our suicide, murder, and human trafficking rates are high among children. As a nation we need to turn our hearts back to God, and God's righteous judgment may be the only solution.

Romans 12:19 says, "Dearly beloved, avenge not yourselves, but rather give place unto wrath: for it is written, Vengeance is mine; I will repay, saith the Lord." (KJV)

Chapter 18
The Coming Famine

Romans 8:35-39 says:

> Who shall separate us from the love of Christ? Shall
> trouble or hardship or persecution or famine or
> nakedness or danger or sword? As it is written:
> "For your sake we face death all day long; we are
> considered as sheep to be slaughtered." No, in all
> these things we are more than conquerors through
> him who loved us. For I am convinced that neither
> death nor life, neither angels nor demons, neither
> the present nor the future, nor any powers, neither
> height nor depth, nor anything else in all creation,
> will be able to separate us from the love of God that
> is in Christ Jesus our Lord. (NIV)

In my prayer time with the Lord, He put on my heart
to prepare for the draught, hyperinflation, and manufac-
tured supply chain shortages that lay ahead, all leading
to famine in America. America's small family farms have

been in deep decline for decades due to stringent laws, competitive pricing due to increased globalization, and corporate farming. According to an article in *Time Magazine,* "The nation lost more than 100,000 farms between 2011 and 2018; 12,000 of those between 2017 and 2018 alone."[29]

Small farmers see the government on the side of large corporate farms like Dupont, Novartis, and Monsanto. "Get big or get out," Earl Butz, Nixon's secretary of agriculture, infamously told farmers in the 1970's. This type of mentality has pushed many small farmers out of business. From 1948 to 2015, nearly 4 million farms have disappeared from the American landscape.

As small farms are closing, land and resources are being bought up by government agencies, corporations, and billionaires like Bill Gates. As these multinational corporations and government agencies come together, they can dictate supply and demand. They can effortlessly manipulate the markets for their political and financial gain. Whoever controls the food and the money supply controls the people. The globalist goal is to transition from relying on ourselves to relying on the government for goods and supplies.

The pandemic further gave governments a window of opportunity to push many Americans out of jobs and onto government aid. Private business owners were forced to close under aggressive emergency orders from governors. Some were even threatened with jail time if they didn't adhere to newly formed directives.

---

29 "'They're Trying to Wipe Us Off the Map.' Small American Farmers Are Nearing Extinction," *Time* article, https://time.com/5736789/small-american-farmers-debt-crisis-extinction/

The Great Reset led by globalists like Claus Schwab and democratic governments around the world are advocating for more reliance on government for daily resources and food. Putting this type of power in the hands of a few corrupt people with self-serving globalist agendas could be catastrophic for the world population. Their overall goal is to collectivize the world under a new global order and power structure.

Claus Schwab asserts the pandemic has forced us to make new moral choices:

> The pandemic has forced all of us, citizens and policy-makers alike, willing, or not, to enter into a philosophical debate about how to maximize the common good in the least damaging way possible. First and foremost, it prompted us to think more deeply about what the common good really means. Common good is that which benefits society as a whole, but how do we decide collectively what is best for society?

His overall goal is to encourage society to think collectively because collective societies are more willing to give power and control into the hands of their elite leaders. The horrors of socialism have been swept neatly under the rug, and globalists around the world continue to promote collective economic agendas controlled by a few.

On a recent trip to Ireland, I learned about the great Irish famine of 1947 that killed approximately 1.5 million people and led to many of the Irish immigrating to America. The population of Ireland still has not reached pre-famine numbers of 8 million people.

The Irish famine was blamed on a bacterium that affected the potato crops, but the potato blight is only half the story. Due to British rule, the impoverished Irish people did not own their own land. The potato was the most nourishing vegetable that could be grown on a small acre. Growing wheat would take four times as much land to feed a family of six. During the worst years of the famine, much of Ireland's produce was exported to England. Even during the peak of the famine, 1 million gallons of butter and 1.7 million gallons of grain alcohol were sent to England. The Irish population did not have access to available food, so they were forced to starve.

In addition, tens of thousands of Irish people were evicted from their homes. Parliament passed a law called The Irish Poor Law, which made Irish landlords responsible for the relief of the poor on their properties, those valued at four pounds or less. This law was a strong incentive for burdened landlords to remove impoverished renters.[30]

According to Josephine Butler, a social reformer in 1846, "When criticism of the evictions reached the British newspapers, Lord Broughman made a speech at the house of Lords: It is the landlord's right to do as he pleases. The tenants must be taught by the strong arm of the law that they have no power to oppose or resist. Sick and aged, little children and women with child, were thrust forth into the snows of winter. And to prevent their return their cabins were levelled to the ground and burned. The few remaining tenants were forbidden to receive the outcast. The majority rendered penniless by the famine wandered aimlessly about the roads or bogs till they found refuge in the workhouse or the grave."[31]

30 *The Truth behind the Irish Famine*, p. 112. Jerry Mulvihill 2020

31 Ibid., 117.

This mass evictions of homes due to a new law that made landlords liable forced families into workhouses set up by the British government. In 1847 nearly 750,000 people were displaced into those workhouses and 3 million Irish people were fed in soup kitchens. Many immigrated and died on "coffin ships," desperate places with nearly-dead passengers. Landlords would sometimes pay to remove a family from their property.

Government relief became available but at a great cost to the Irish farmers. A law was passed called the Quarter Acre Clause, "Whereby any farmer wishing to obtain outdoor relief, that is, food for his wife, children, and himself had to first to surrender all rights to any land over and above one quarter of a stature acre."[32]

I had the opportunity to visit the famine cabins near the coast of Ireland. This is an educational site to honor those lost during this difficult time. These cabins educated the public about the harsh conditions these impoverished people lived under. As I approached a cabin on top of a large hill, someone retrieving a free-roaming young, black sheep that had escaped its fenced yard greeted me at the entrance.

I had seen many sheep on this weeklong trip, but this was the first black sheep I had encountered. It was an additional sign from the Lord that famine is in our near future. The black horse in the book of Revelation is a sign of famine. I don't discount these small encounters because every encounter is significant to someone led by the Holy Spirit. This little sheep was terribly cute, but I couldn't help but hear its soft cry as a cry of coming distress. I pray

---

32 Ibid., 151.

that when difficult times come, we are more prepared than these poor people were in recent history.

America's access to small family-owned farms allowed many people to survive the Great Depression of 1929, resulting in massive unemployment. While many rural families farmed their small acre of land to ensure they had enough food, families in cities were significantly more dependent on government aid. America's dependency on corporate farms makes our population much more at risk of supply shortages.

America's move toward corporate farming has been at a lengthy pace, but it has been similarly impactful in moving land from small family farms to large corporate farms that are more easily controlled by government policy. This increase in corporate farms puts the control of America's food supply in the hands of fewer large corporations.

The push toward urban migration because of increased globalization has left many small towns empty and struggling to survive. According to an article in Time Magazine, "Around 4,400 schools in rural districts closed between 2011 and 2015, the most recent year for which there is data available, according to the National Center for Education Statistics; suburban districts, by contrast, added roughly 4,000 schools over that same time period."[33]

If Americans need to return to farming, there may not be any farmland available. Business owners like Bill Gates are now the largest private landowners in America. Native American professor Nick Estes stated in a recent *Guardian* article, "He now owns more farmland than my entire Native American nation.... In total, Gates owns approximately 242,000 acres of farmland with assets totaling more than

33 "'They're Trying to Wipe Us Off the Map.' Small American Farmers Are Nearing Extinction," *Time* article, https://time.com/5736789/small-american-farmers-debt-crisis-extinction/

$690m.... To put that in perspective, that's nearly the size of Hong Kong, and twice the acreage of the Lower Brule Sioux Tribe, where I'm an enrolled member," Estes said.[34]

Having influential billionaires like Bill Gates owning such large percentages of land can have a significant impact on the food markets and future trends. Gates has openly advocated for eating 100 percent synthetic beef. When asked during an interview with *MIT's Technology Review* how to cut back on methane emissions, Gates replied, "I do think all rich countries should move to 100 percent synthetic beef....You can get used to the taste difference, and the claim is they're going to make it taste even better over time. Eventually, that green premium is modest enough that you can sort of change the [behavior of] people or use regulation to totally shift the demand.[35]

Another concern is the increase of fires and tragedies at American food distribution plants in 2021 and 2022, most of which came after President Biden announced that food prices would significantly increase. Biden said at NATO Headquarters in Brussels on March, 24, 2022, "We had a long discussion in the G7 with the, with both the United States, which has a significant — the third-largest producer of wheat in the world — as well as Canada, which is

34 "Bill Gates is the biggest private owner of farmland in the United States. Why?" *Guardian* article by Nick Estes, April 5, 2021. https://www.theguardian.com/commentisfree/2021/apr/05/bill-gates-climate-crisis-farmland

35 "Bill Gates thinks we should start eating '100% synthetic beef'," *New York Post* article by Lia Eustachewich, February 16, 2021, https://nypost.com/2021/02/16/bill-gates-thinks-we-should-start-eating-synthetic-beef/

also a major, major producer, and we both talked about how we could increase and disseminate more rapidly food, food shortages."[36]

Following is a list of the fires targeted at food processing plants across America, compiled by Israel 365 News:

- In the middle of the night on March 23, a fire broke out on the roof of the General Mills food processing plant in Cedar Rapids, Iowa.

- On March 28, Maricopa Food Pantry, a local food bank in Arizona, lost 50,000 pounds worth of food in a fire that occurred "just 15 minutes after their food bank closed," according to a CBS affiliate. Arizona's Family. AZCentral cited CEO Jim Shoaf, who said that 15,000 pounds of meat and 40,000 pounds of canned goods and "other commodities" were lost in the blaze.

- On March 31, a structure fire significantly damaged a large portion of the Rio Fresh onion packing facility in San Juan, Texas. It was the largest fresh onion packing facility in the region.

- On April 12, a major fire broke out at New Hampshire's East Conway Beef and Pork slaughterhouse.

- On April 13, the Taylor Farms California Foodservice production facility in Salinas, California, burned almost entirely to the ground. The facility employed nearly 1,000 people. An update on the company's website described the Salinas facility as its primary production facility.

---

36 "25 Mysterious Fires at Food Processing Plants Across US; 'End-of-Days Food Shortage'," *Israel 365* News article by Adam Eliyahu Berkowitz, May 2, 2022, https://www.israel365news.com/268985/25-mysterious-fires-at-food-processing-plants-across-us-end-of-days-food-shortage/

- On April 14, a small plane crashed into the Gem State food processing plant in Heyburn, Idaho. The website for the company describes itself as processing 18,000 acres worth of potatoes each year.
- On April 19, the headquarters of Azure Standard, the nation's premier independent distributor of organic and healthy food, was destroyed by fire. The company released a statement that due to the destruction, the company "will experience out-of-stock status for Azure Market oils, honey, and vinegar – basically any Azure Market liquid product – as well as our carob products for the short term." The destruction may also affect product supplies from their fruit packing facility.
- On March 24, 2022, a fire destroyed the Penobscot McCrum potato processing plant in Belfast, Maine.
- On March 16, 2022, according to KAIT, a fire caused extensive damage to a new production line dedicated to Hot Pockets at a Nestle plant in Jonesboro, Arkansas.
- On March 16, a major fire hit the 1.2 million-square-foot Walmart fulfillment center in Plainfield, Indiana.
- On February 22, 2022, a propane boiler explosion caused a fire that destroyed the Shearer's Foods potato chip plant in Northeast Oregon.
- On February 3, 2022, according to NBC15 in Madison, Wisconsin, a fire destroyed part of the Wisconsin River Meats site in Mauston.
- On January 13, 2022, according to KALB, an explosion and fire damaged the Cargill-Nutrena plant in Lecompte, Louisiana.

- On January 6, 2022, a fire did extensive damage to a poultry processing plant in Hamilton, Ontario, according to CHCH-TV.
- On December 13, 2021, a fire broke out at a food processing plant in San Antonio, Texas. When firefighters arrived on the scene, they found a freezer on fire in the facility. $150,000 worth of food was destroyed in the fire.
- On November 29, 2021, a fire broke out at the Maid-Rite Steak Company meat processing plant in Scott Township, Lackawanna County, Pennsylvania. The cause of this fire has been ruled an accident.
- On September 12, 2021, a fire broke out at the JVS USA beef processing plant in Grand Island, Nebraska. According to Drovers, the nation's oldest livestock publication, the fire was determined to be from a heater near the roof in the rendering area of the plant.
- On August 23, 2021, a fire broke out at Patak Meat Products in Cobb County, Georgia. In March of 2022, the company said on Facebook that it is still rebuilding.
- On July 31, 2021, according to WVTM, the NBC station in Birmingham, Alabama, a fire broke out at Tyson's River Valley Ingredients rendering plant in Hanceville, Alabama.
- On July 25, 2021, a fire damaged a Kellogg's plant in Memphis, Tennessee. According to fire officials, it was accidentally set off when a malfunctioning conveyer belt sparked a blaze in a rice drying machine.
- On April 30, 2021, a fire broke out at the Smithfield Foods pork processing plant in Monmouth, Illinois.

- On January 11, 2021, a fire destroyed the Deli Star meat processing plant in Fayetteville, Illinois, according to Meat+Poultry.[37]

Thegatewaypundit.com included an additional list of tragedies at food processing plants in the last year. These included meat that was being destroyed over concerns of bird flu. These abundant incidents will surely lead to an increase in national prices, sending inflation even higher.

1. 1/11/21 A fire that destroyed a 75,000-square-foot processing plant in Fayetteville.
2. 4/30/21 A fire ignited inside the Smithfield Foods pork processing plant in Monmouth, Illinois.
3. 7/25/21 Three-alarm fire at Kellogg plant in Memphis;170 emergency personnel responded to the call.
4. 7/30/21 Firefighters battled a large fire at Tyson's River Valley Ingredients plant in Hanceville, Alabama.
5. 8/23/21 Fire crews were called to the Patak Meat Production company on Ewing Road in Austell.
6. 9/13/21 A fire at the JBS beef plant in Grand Island, Nebraska, forced a halt to slaughter and fabrication lines.
7. 10/13/21 A five-alarm fire ripped through the Darigold butter production plant in Caldwell, Idaho.
8. 11/15/21 A woman is in custody following a fire at the Garrard County Food Pantry.
9. 11/29/21 A fire broke out around 5:30 p.m. at the Maid-Rite Steak Company meat processing plant.

---

37 Ibid.

10. 12/13/21 West Side food processing plant in San Antonio left with smoke damage after a fire.

11. 1/7/22 Damage to a poultry processing plant on Hamilton's Mountain following an overnight fire.

12. 1/13/22 Firefighters worked for 12 hours to put a fire out at the Cargill-Nutrena plant in Lecompte, Louisiana.

13. 1/31/22 a fertilizer plant with 600 tons of ammonium nitrate inside caught on fire on Cherry Street in Winston-Salem, North Carolina.

14. 2/3/22 A massive fire swept through Wisconsin River Meats in Mauston.

15. 2/3/22 At least 130 cows were killed in a fire at Percy Farm in Stowe.

16. 2/15/22 Bonanza Meat Company goes up in flames in El Paso, Texas.

17. 2/15/22 Nearly a week after the fire destroyed most of the Shearer's Foods plant in Hermiston.

18. 2/16/22 A fire broke out at the U.S.'s largest soybean processing and biodiesel plant in Claypool, Indiana.

19. 2/18/22 An early morning fire tore through the milk parlor at Bess View Farm.

20. 2/19/22 Three people were injured, and one was hospitalized, after an ammonia leak at Lincoln Premium Poultry in Fremont.

21. 2/22/22 The Shearer's Foods plant in Hermiston caught fire after a propane boiler exploded.

22. 2/28/22 A smoldering pile of sulfur quickly became a raging chemical fire at Nutrien Ag Solutions.

23. 2/28/22 A man was hurt after a fire broke out at the Shadow Brook Farm and Dutch Girl Creamery.

24. 3/4/22 294,800 chickens were destroyed at a farm in Stoddard, Missouri.
25. 3/4/22 644,000 chickens were destroyed at an egg farm in Cecil, Maryland.
26. 3/8/22 243,900 chickens were destroyed at an egg farm in New Castle, Delaware.
27. 3/10/22 663,400 chickens were destroyed at an egg farm in Cecil, Maryland.
28. 3/10/22 915,900 chickens were destroyed at an egg farm in Taylor, Iowa.
29. 3/14/22 The blaze at 244 Meadow Drive was discovered shortly after 5 p.m. by farm owner Wayne Hoover.
30. 3/14/22 2,750,700 chickens were destroyed at an egg farm in Jefferson, Wisconsin.
31. 3/16/22 A fire at a Walmart warehouse distribution center has cast a large plume of smoke visible throughout Indianapolis.
32. 3/16/22 Nestle Food Plant was extensively damaged in a fire and new production was destroyed in Jonesboro, Arkansas.
33. 3/17/22 5,347,500 chickens were destroyed at an egg farm in Buena Vista, Iowa.
34. 3/17/22 147,600 chickens were destroyed at an farm in Kent, Delaware.
35. 3/18/22 315,400 chickens were destroyed at an egg farm in Cecil, Maryland.
36. 3/22/22 172,000 turkeys were destroyed on farms in South Dakota.
37. 3/22/22 570,000 chickens were destroyed at a farm in Butler, Nebraska.
38. 3/24/22 Firefighters from numerous towns battled a major fire at the McCrum potato processing facility in Belfast.

39. 3/24/22 418,500 chickens were destroyed at a farm in Butler, Nebraska.
40. 3/25/22 250,300 chickens were destroyed at an egg farm in Franklin, Iowa.
41. 3/26/22 311,000 turkeys were destroyed in Minnesota.
42. 3/27/22 126,300 turkeys were destroyed in South Dakota.
43. 3/28/22 1,460,000 chickens were destroyed at an egg farm in Guthrie, Iowa.
44. 3/29/22 A massive fire burned 40,000 pounds of food meant to feed people in a food desert near Maricopa.
45. 3/31/22 A structure fire caused significant damage to a large portion of key fresh onion packing facilities in South Texas.
46. 3/31/22 76,400 turkeys were destroyed in Osceola, Iowa.
47. 3/31/22 5,011,700 chickens were destroyed at an egg farm in Osceola, Iowa.
48. 4/6/22 281,600 chickens were destroyed at a farm in Wayne, North Carolina.
49. 4/9/22 76,400 turkeys were destroyed in Minnesota.
50. 4/9/22 208,900 turkeys were destroyed in Minnesota.
51. 4/12/22 89,700 chickens were destroyed at a farm in Wayne, North Carolina.
52. 4/12/22 1,746,900 chickens were destroyed at an egg farm in Dixon, Nebraska.
53. 4/12/22 259,000 chickens were destroyed at a farm in Minnesota.

54. 4/13/22 fire destroys East Conway Beef & Pork Meat Market in Conway, New Hampshire.
55. 4/13/22 plane crashes into Gem State Processing, an Idaho potato and food processing plant.
56. 4/13/22 77,000 turkeys were destroyed in Minnesota.
57. 4/14/22 Taylor Farms Food Processing plant burns down Salinas, California.
58. 4/14/22 99,600 turkeys destroyed in Minnesota.
59. 4/15/22 1,380,500 chickens destroyed at an egg farm in Lancaster, Minnesota.
60. 4/19/22 Azure Standard, the nation's premier independent distributor of organic and healthy food, was destroyed by fire in Dufur, Oregon.
61. 4/19/22 339,000 turkeys were destroyed in Minnesota.
62. 4/19/22 58,000 chickens were destroyed at a farm in Montrose, Colorado.
63. 4/20/22 2,000,000 chickens were destroyed at an egg farm in Minnesota.
64. 4/21/22 a small plane crashed in the lot of a General Mills plant in Georgia.
65. 4/22/22 197,000 turkeys were destroyed in Minnesota.
66. 4/23/22 200,000 turkeys were destroyed in Minnesota.
67. 4/25/22 1,501,200 chickens were destroyed at an egg farm in Cache, Utah.
68. 4/26/22 307,400 chickens were destroyed at a farm in Lancaster, Pennsylvania.
69. 4/27/22 2,118,000 chickens were destroyed at a farm in Knox, Nebraska.

70. 4/28/22 egg-laying facility in Iowa kills 5.3 million chickens, fires 200-plus workers.
71. 4/28/22 Allen Harim Foods processing plant killed nearly 2M chickens in Delaware.
72. 4/2822 110,700 turkeys destroyed in Barron, Wisconsin.
73. 4/29/22 1,366,200 chickens were destroyed at a farm in Weld, Colorado.
74. 4/30/22 13,800 chickens were destroyed at a farm in Sequoia, Oklahoma.
75. 5/3/22 58,000 turkeys were destroyed in Barron, Wisconsin.
76. 5/3/22 118,900 turkeys were destroyed in Beadle, Southa Dakota.
77. 5/3/22 114,000 ducks were destroyed at a duck farm in Berks, Pennsylvania.
78. 5/3/22 118,900 turkeys were destroyed in Lyon, Minnesota.
79. 5/7/22 20,100 turkeys were destroyed in Barron, Wisconsin.
80. 5/10/22 72,300 chickens were destroyed at a farm in Lancaster, Pennsylvania.
81. 5/10/22 61,000 ducks were destroyed at a duck farm in Berks, Pennsylvania.
82. 5/10/22 35,100 turkeys were destroyed in Muskegon, Michigan.
83. 5/13/22 10,500 turkeys were destroyed in Barron, Wisconsin.
84. 5/14/22 83,400 ducks were destroyed at a duck farm in Berks, Pennsylvania.
85. 5/17/22 79,000 chickens were destroyed at a duck farm in Berks, Pennsylvania.

86. 5/18/22 7,200 ducks were destroyed at a duck farm in Berks, Pennsylvania.
87. 5/19/22 train carrying limestone derailed in Jensen Beach, Florida.
88. 5/21/22 57,000 turkeys were destroyed on a farm in Dakota, Minnesota.
89. 5/23/22 4,000 ducks were destroyed at a duck farm in Berks, Pennsylvania.
90. 5/29/22 a Saturday-night fire destroyed a poultry building at Forsman Farms.
91. 5/31/22 3,000,000 chickens were destroyed by fire at Forsman facility in Stockholm Township, Minnesota.
92. 6/2/22 30,000 ducks were destroyed at a duck farm in Berks, Pennsylvania.
93. 6/7/22 a fire occurred at the JBS meat packing plant in Green Bay, Wisconsin.
94. 6/8/22 firefighters from Tangipahoa Fire District 1 responded to a fire at the Purina Feed Mill in Arcola.
95. 6/9/22 irrigation water was canceled in Commie, California (the #1 producer of food in the U.S.) and storage water was flushed directly out to the delta.
96. 6/12/22 largest pork company in the U.S. shuts down Commie, California, plant due to high costs
97. 6/13/22 fire breaks out at a food processing plant west of Waupaca County in Wisconsin.[38]

All these things happening in our world can leave us feeling hopeless, but our future is found in God. Our world systems may be crashing before our eyes, but the

---

38 https://www.thegatewaypundit.com/2022/06/another-closure-one-largest-chicken-producers-u-s-announces-tennessee-plant-shutdown/ By Jim Hoft, Published June 26, 2022 at 6:42pm

faithful can trust in the supernatural provision of God to provide during difficult times. Psalm 37:25 says, "I have been young, and now am old; yet have I not seen the righteous forsaken, nor his seed begging bread." (KJV) Even in my early years when my mother had limited funds to provide for us, we never went hungry. God continued to help us in our time of need.

We need to put all our hope and trust in Jesus to be ready for the days of travail that will quickly come upon the Earth. Ask God to strengthen your faith today so that you can walk in supernatural security. Build your foundation on the rock, who is Christ Jesus. Matthew 6:25-26 says:

> Therefore I tell you, do not worry about your life, what you will eat or drink; or about your body, what you will wear. Is not life more than food, and the body more than clothes? Look at the birds of the air; they do not sow or reap or store away in barns, and yet your heavenly Father feeds them. Are you not much more valuable than they? (NIV)

You and your family are valuable to God! Ask the Lord to lead you in preparation for difficult times. We need to put all our trust in Jesus.

Chapter 19
The Golden Calf

Exodus 32:1-4 says:

> When the people saw that Moses was so long in com-
> ing down from the mountain, they gathered around
> Aaron and said, "Come, make us gods who will go be-
> fore us. As for this fellow Moses who brought us up out
> of Egypt, we don't know what has happened to him."
>
> Aaron answered them, "Take off the gold ear-
> rings that your wives, your sons and your daugh-
> ters are wearing, and bring them to me." So all the
> people took off their earrings and brought them to
> Aaron. He took what they handed him and made it
> into an idol cast in the shape of a calf, fashioning it
> with a tool. Then they said, "These are your gods,
> Israel, who brought you up out of Egypt." (NIV)

In the absence of their leader, Moses, the Israelites decided to replace the God of their ancestors with a golden

calf, made in the image of their preference. They even declared, "This is your God, Israel, that brought you out of Egypt."

Sadly, many of us trust also in the world's system instead of the God of our salvation. We trust in our retirement accounts and our own ability to plan and provide for the future. America as a nation has certainly worshipped the golden calf of prosperity instead of the dedicated allegiance to our biblical heritage.

The American dollar and the American stock market have been long standing golden calves. American Presidents share their success by exalting the bull markets and blaming the previous administration for past bear markets. We trust in the market's ability to progressively climb over time and add prosperity to prosperity. We are taught that if you don't put all your eggs in one financial basket, you will surely do well in the end.

The last seventy-five years proves this way of thinking well, because overall America has been affluent. But the coming turbulence will shift our trust from the American dollar and the financial market back to the living God. Zephaniah 1:18 says, "Neither their silver nor their gold will be able to save them on the day of the LORD's wrath. In the fire of his jealousy the whole earth will be consumed, for he will make a sudden end of all who live on the earth." (NIV)

In previous chapters, I discussed the enormous debt the American government continues to accumulate and how this will likely lead to the collapse of the dollar. We are nearly 30 trillion dollars in debt as of 2022, meaning each American citizen owes approximately $290K in U.S. debt accrued by our government. The federal reserve continues to print money with no regard for the cash to ever be returned. This insensible spending is a strategy to bring us into a new global monetary system.

When our monetary system fails, our nation will be looking for ways to restore our way of life and prosperity. This new system will be regulated and controlled by a new global hierarchy that will track our spending and allegiance to their sustainability goals. The Bible refers to this global monetary system as the beast system, which will cause both the prosperous and the poor to take a mark on the right hand or the forehead to be able to buy or sell. Revelation 13:16-18 says:

> It also forced all people, great and small, rich and poor, free and slave, to receive a mark on their right hands or on their foreheads, so that they could not buy or sell unless they had the mark, which is the name of the beast or the number of its name. This calls for wisdom. Let the person who has insight calculate the number of the beast, for it is the number of a man. That number is 666. (NIV)

The number six is the number of man, because man was created on the sixth day. The number 666 could represent the reign of man instead of the heavenly reign of God. The Bible gives many prophetic clues that are continuously unfolding.

The IMF and the global banking system have been working tirelessly on initiatives that would allow for all people to be included in a world banking system. An article by the American Institute for Economic Research says, "Financial inclusion has become a top priority for international agencies like the World Bank and the IMF, as well as for nonprofits like the Bill and Melinda Gates Foundation, which also has donated millions to fund financial inclusion initiatives across the world."[39]

Inclusion also means that everyone on this global system will be monitored by the new global authorities. Global companies have put a plan into action to create ID 2020, the founding partners of which include the Rockefeller Foundation, Gavi (the vaccine alliance), and Microsoft. Global banks see this ID implemented in the next few years. ID 2020 is centered on identifying a person based on biometrics, an eye scan, fingerprints, as well as face and voice.

The global beast system is strongly connected to the money supply. The American dollar denotes its occultic loyalty. In *The Secret Destiny of America*, author Manly P. Hall unfolds the meaning behind the symbolism of the American dollar:

> For more than three thousand years, secret societies have labored to create the background of knowledge necessary to establish an enlightened democracy among the nations of the world. Men bound by a secret oath to labor in the cause of world democracy decided that in the American colonies they would plant the roots of a new way of life. Brotherhoods were established to meet secretly, and they quietly and industriously conditioned America to its destiny for leadership in a free world.

39 "Banking the Unbanked: Lessons from the Developing World," an American Institute for Economic Research article by Scott A. Burns, February 29, 2020, https://www.aier.org/article/banking-the-unbanked-lessons-from-the-developing-world/

On the reverse of our nation's Great Seal is an unfinished pyramid to represent human society itself, imperfect and incomplete. Above floats the symbol of the esoteric order, the radiant triangle with its all-seeing eye.... There is only one possible origin for these symbols, and that is the secret societies which came to this country 150 years before the Revolutionary War.[40]

Many Americans would be shocked to learn that a small group of international bankers connected to secret societies control our federal reserve system. The Owen-Glass act, creating the federal reserve system, was passed through Congress on December 23, 1913. The act was cleverly positioned to be heard during the Christmas holiday since many of the politicians would be home with their families.

But Ezekiel 7:9 warns, "They will throw their silver into the streets, and their gold will be treated as a thing unclean. Their silver and gold will not be able to deliver them in the day of the LORD's wrath. It will not satisfy their hunger or fill their stomachs, for it has caused them to stumble into sin." (NIV)

---

40 Manly P. Hall, *The Secret Destiny of America,* The Philosophical Research Society, Inc., Los Angeles, California, 1944, p. 72.

Chapter 20
The Globalist Agenda

The journey of the one world government, one world religion, and one world economy date back to the tower of Babel in the plain of Shinar. Mankind, in its desire to reach the heavens for the purpose of prestige, decided to unite as one. The people's hearts were not centered on God's will but on their own ambitions. Genesis 11:1-8 says:

> Now the whole world had one language and a common speech. As people moved eastward, they found a plain in Shinar and settled there. They said to each other, "Come, let's make bricks and bake them thoroughly." They used brick instead of stone, and tar for mortar. Then they said, "Come, let us build ourselves a city, with a tower that reaches to the heavens, so that we may make a name for ourselves; otherwise we will be scattered over the face of the whole earth." (NIV)

But the LORD came down to see the city and the tower the people were building. The LORD said, "If as one people speaking the same language they have begun to do this, then nothing they plan to do will be impossible for them. Come, let us go down and confuse their language so they will not understand each other."

So the LORD scattered them from there over all the earth, and they stopped building the city.

God's ultimate goal is to bring His glorious Kingdom to earth, but mankind has been centered on building its own kingdoms that testify to its achievements and ability. Jesus revealed that He has always been centered on doing what He saw His Heavenly Father doing, His heart completely aligned with Heaven's purpose. This is the model for Christians today and reiterated in Jesus' model prayer for the disciples in Matthew 6:9-13:

> "Our Father in heaven, Hallowed be Your name. Your kingdom come. Your will be done On earth as *it is* in heaven. Give us this day our daily bread. And forgive us our debts, As we forgive our debtors. And do not lead us into temptation, But deliver us from the evil one. For Yours is the kingdom and the power and the glory forever. Amen." (NKJV)

God's perfect plan will be established at the second coming of Jesus the Messiah, and His Messianic reign is disclosed in the book of Revelation.

The devil also saw the hearts of mankind, and he played with their desire for power and prestige to turn man against God. Global domination has a rich history in the hearts of mankind. The desire for global control of the masses has been an inner desire for many tyrants of previous ages, but this current age of technology offers the unique resources necessary for power and control.

The globalist agenda is predicated on controlling the world's population and resources. Their attempt to do this starts with telling people the world will run out of resources and enter a cycle of global disaster that is irreversible unless there is new global ordinance and shift from global resources to global powers.

Organizations like the World Economic Forum, Counsel for Foreign Relations, and the United Nations are pushing the globalist socialist agenda that we all must come together and do our part or the planet will not survive. They further warn that humans are the Earth's biggest problem, and we need to depopulate by eliminating anyone who descents from strict climate policies.

According to a 2019 article in *BioScience,* more than 11,000 scientists say the world is "still increasing by roughly 80 million people per year, or more than 200,000 per day," so "the world population must be stabilized—and, ideally, gradually reduced."[41] This shows there is considerable ambition from the scientific community to encourage family planning to reduce the overall birth rate. This type of thinking will inevitability prioritize the planet over the needs of humans, which can lead to eugenics, racism, and dehumanization of anyone who does not share the same beliefs as the majority.

In a 1991 article titled, "The Population Control Agenda," Dr. Stanley Monteith lays out his deep concerns about

---

41 *BioScience,* Volume 70, Issue 1, January 2020, Pages 8-12, https://doi.org/10.1093/biosci/biz088. The article was originally published on November 5, 2019, but *Bioscience* has since removed the original article due to backlash.

a coming new world order headed by the United Nations and World Bank. This new order will control the water supply and have authority over all natural resources.

Dr. Monteith had been studying the creation of a global government for more than fifty years, and his work as an orthopedic surgeon informed him of the coming world order. He wrote many books and created a radio station to release this timeless message. He has left us a legacy of information to learn from of how the coming new world order plans to take control. Specifically, he warns of a plan of global government and depopulation. When asked why he believed such things, he responded with:

> The answer is quite simple: I have read the writings of those who intend to depopulate large segments of the earth and I believe them. They have written of the necessity of reducing—by force if necessary—the world's population.

In the November 1991 issue of the *UNESCO Courier*, Jacques Cousteau wrote:

> The damage people cause to the planet is a function of demographics—it is equal to the degree of development. One American burdens the Earth much more than twenty Bangladeshes.... This is a terrible thing to say. In order to stabilize world population, we must eliminate 350,000 people per day. It is a horrible thing to say, but it's just as bad not to say it.[42]

---

42 "The Population Controllers," *New American Magazine*, 6/27/94, p. 7.

The September 1, 1997, issue of *National Review* magazine, tells us:

A small cadre of obscure international bureaucrats are hard at work devising a system of "global governance" that is slowly gaining control over ordinary Americans' lives. Maurice Strong, a sixty-eight-year-old Canadian, is the "indispensable man" at the center of this creeping UN power grab.

Dr. Stanley Monteith explains that Maurice Strong, the founding Executive Director of the UN Environment Programme (UNEP) and the pioneer of global sustainable development, is a leader of the secret world of corporate finance and is currently the primary force behind the UN plan to establish a world government. According to Monteith's website:

Strong will forever be remembered for placing the environment on the international agenda and at the heart of development. He shepherded global environmental governance processes — from the original Rio Earth Summit, Agenda 21 and the Rio Declaration to the launch of the UN Framework Convention on Climate Change and the Convention on Biological Diversity.... This is not just a technical issue. Everybody's actions are motivated by their inner life, their moral, spiritual and ethical values. Global agreements will be effective when they are rooted in the individual commitment of people, which arises from their own inner life.[43]

---

43 "The World Mourns One of its Greats: Maurice Strong Dies, His Legacy Lives On," http://www.mauricestrong.net/index.php/earth-summit-strong

Strong promoted UN global policies that were closely tied to the message of the Georgia Guidestones, world
government, new age religion, and environmentalism.

In 1990, Daniel Wood interviewed Maurice Strong
and wrote an article based on his encounter, published
in *West* magazine in May of 1990. He said that Strong:

> ...presented the idea that the only way to save the
> planet from destruction is to see to it that the in-
> dustrialized civilizations collapse.... What if a small
> group of ... world leaders were to conclude that the
> principal risk to the earth comes from the actions
> of the rich countries? And if the world is to survive,
> those rich countries would have to sign an agree-
> ment reducing their impact on the environment
> will they do it? .... The group's conclusion is "no," so
> in order to save the planet, the group decides: isn't
> the only hope for the planet that the industrialized
> civilizations collapse. Isn't it our responsibility to
> bring that about?... Maurice Strong, and the occul-
> tic force he represents, intends to establish a world
> government, enslave all mankind, and destroy Ju-
> deo-Christian civilization. Mr. Strong admits that he
> is a dedicated socialist, he believes in authoritarian
> rule of the masses.[44]

Monteith also says:

> The Occult Hierarchy which controls both the
> radical left and the environmental movement now
> intend to destroy American agriculture, take away
> our automobiles, further restrict private property

---

44 *West* magazine, 1990, p. 9-12.

rights, deindustrialize America, and destroy Christianity. If my allegations seem too far-fetched to believe, I suggest that you read the summary of the Global Biodiversity Assessment report.[45]

Some elitists see humanity as a plague on the Earth's ecosystem. Their overall goal is to work to decrease the world population and to reduce the effects of the virus called humanity.

David Graber, a research biologist with the National Park Service, was quoted in the October 22, 1989 *Los Angeles Times* book review section as saying:

> Human happiness and certainly human fecundity are not as important as a wild and healthy planet. I know social scientists who remind me that people are part of nature, but it isn't true... We have become a plague upon ourselves and upon the Earth.... Until such time as homosapiens should decide to rejoin nature, some of us can only hope for the right virus to come along.[46]

In *The First Global Revolution,* published by the Council of the Club of Rome, an international elitist organization, the authors note that, "In searching for a new enemy to unite us, we came up with the idea that pollution, the threat of global warming, water shortages, famine, and the like would fit the bill. All these dangers are caused by human intervention...."

---

45 *Sustainable Development: An Expose of the Origins and goals of Modern-Day Environmentalism,* Extracts from Dr. Stanley Monteith's book..., Endtimes Ministries, Christian Resource Centre http://www.despatch.cth.com.au/Books_V/sustainDevBKredone.pdf

46 *Los Angeles Times,* Book Review Section, October 22, 1989, p. 9.

The real enemy, then, is humanity itself."[47]

On April 5, 1994, the *Los Angeles Times* quoted Cornell University Professor David Pimentel, speaking to the American Association for the Advancement of Science, as saying, "The total world population should be no more than 2 billion rather than the current 5.6 billion."

In *The Impact of Science on Society*, Bertrand Russell said:

> At present the population of the world is increasing.... War so far has had no great effect on this increase.... I do not pretend that birth control is the only way in which population can be kept from increasing. There are others.... If a Black Death could be spread throughout the world once in every generation, survivors could procreate freely without making the world too full...the state of affairs might be somewhat unpleasant, but what of it? Really high-minded people are indifferent to suffering, especially that of others.

Negative Population Growth Inc. of Teaneck, New Jersey, recently circulated a letter stating their long-range goal: "We believe that our goal for the United States should be no more than 150 million; our size in 1950. For the world, we believe our goal should be a population of not more than two billion, its size shortly after the turn of the century."[48]

---

47   *The First Global Revolution: Club of Rome,* Alexander King and Bertrand Schneider, Pantheon Books, New York, 1991, p. 115.

48   Material is available from Radio Liberty, P.O. Box 13, Santa Cruz, CA, 95063.

As we can see, decreasing the world's population has been a shared opinion in scientific and elite circles. World influencers like Bill Gates, whose father was on the board of Planned Parenthood, have spoken about the need to control population growth, but some of these opinions have been silenced in the aftermath of COVID. Some speculate the COVID virus was manmade to reduce an overpopulated Earth.

Chapter 21
Political Corruption Pushing the Globalist Agenda

Psalm 2:1-6 says:

> Why do the nations conspire and the peoples plot in vain? The kings of the earth rise up and the rulers band together against the Lord and against his anointed, saying, "Let us break their chains and throw off their shackles." The One enthroned in heaven laughs; the Lord scoffs at them. He rebukes them in his anger and terrifies them in his wrath, saying, "I have installed my king on Zion, my holy mountain." (NIV)

The 2020 election was faced with unprecedented global situations, deep political conspiracies, fake news, censorship, and blatant attacks on liberty. As an American, I had heard of about the deep political corruption in Haiti, Brazil, Venezuela, and Mexico, but I had not seen such an obvious display on American soil.

There have always been secret agendas, political partnerships, and special interest groups pushing legislation
and elections, but the 2020 election had an ungodly alignment of media, government agencies, social media, and big
business working congruently to remove President Trump
from office. Their desire was so great that their tactics became sloppy and evident to the viewing audience. The blatant corruption of our politicians and those in the public
sphere is an additional sign of a nation under judgment.

I first want to note the false allegation that Trump had
connections with Russia and stole the 2016 election. Media
outlets ran with the story. In fact, ABC news had an in-depth,
three-part series, initiated by the Hillary Clinton campaign
to lead the public to believe that Trump was compromised
by the Russian government. After an investigation, we now
know the Russian informant, Danchenko, along with two
others, were lying about Trump's involvement.

The FBI received information directly from the Hilary
campaign, via Michael Sussmann, linking Trump to a Russian
bank. The thirty-nine-page dossier that accused Trump of illegal activities was built on exaggerations, lies, and rumors.
The FBI was found negligent in accepting faulty information
as fact and further pushing the Russian narrative. Michael
was later charged with lying to the FBI about his relationship
to the Hilary campaign. In hindsight we see the Hilary campaign, the FBI, and the media were working collectively to
remove President Trump from office.

Trump's director of National Security noted that two
top FBI intelligence agents knew from the start that "Rus-
sian-gate" was a con and decided to prolong the corrupt
media narrative. Two journalists from ABC were even giv-
en a Pulitzer Prize for pushing this discredited story.

This blatant attack on the 45th President of the United States is still being investigated to bring criminal charges against the accusers, but the damage is already done.

Meanwhile, the media silenced evidence of Hunter Biden's covert business dealings in the Ukraine and China until after the 2020 election. John Paul Mac Isaac, a computer shop owner in Delaware, turned over to the FBI legitimate information regarding Hunter Biden's unscrupulous dealings on his laptop. Some of the damning information were emails showing favoritism and bribery to business owners in the Ukraine and China. These emails referred to President Joe Biden as the "Big Guy" in an attempt to protect his identity and involvement. One email from 2017 outlines a deal between the Biden family and a now non-operational Chinese energy company.

The original email was sent by Hunter Biden's business partner, James Gillar, referencing a 10 percent credit to the "Big Guy." A second recipient on the email, Tony Boublinski, an additional business partner of Hunter Biden, later confirmed this email as a legitimate deal. In a media interview, Boublinski mentioned the email and explained that Hunter commonly referred to his father as the "Big Guy" during business dealings. He further explained that Hunter and Joe Biden were paranoid about keeping Joe Biden's involvement secret.

The liberal media outlets including National Public Radio (NPR) discredited the laptop as Russian disinformation, hoping to silence allegations. NPR labeled this important news about Joe Biden's overseas business dealings as a pure distraction that they refused to cover. Additionally, Twitter and Facebook did not allow an official story by the *New York Post* about the Biden laptop to be posted because it didn't align with their desired candidate. Isaac is now suing the media and others involved for defaming his character and his business in a plot to silence the truth.

During my 2020 run for Congress, an immigrant from former communist Romania, and one of my supporters, informed me that in his opinion, the American media was worse than communist propaganda and completely fraudulent.

We are experiencing an unholy alliance of mass media, social media, government agencies, national and international, global corporations, and global leaders coming together to bring the world into a global socialist society under new constitutions that will be managed by a select group of people. Our national struggles are no longer between communism and democracy. It is a division between nationalist and globalist, those who want to continue with a sovereign national model under our current Constitution, and those who want to gain more power and more control under new global contracts. These new contracts will leave the American people in a desperate situation at the mercy of global leaders, and all our God-given rights will be erased.

During the 2020 election, the COVID closures brought in a whole new method of mass mail-in ballots that left considerably more room for error and fraudulent activity. Governors used their emergency powers to seize control of public and private businesses. Michigan's Governor Whitmer loved to throw accusations of racism at anyone who opposed her strict stay-at-home orders. Democrat politicians accused Republicans of trying to kill their grandparents if they went out of their homes, all the while Democrat Governor Whitmer was placing COVID patients in eldercare homes, leading to increased deaths among the elderly.

On January 13, 2022, Fox News wrote, "Michigan state Rep. Steven Johnson, a Republican, told Fox News Digital in a Thursday phone call that Whitmer is "well known" for her executive order "to place COVID-positive patients into nursing homes."[49]

The Michigan Governor later refused to disclose the increased deaths that resulted from this controversial policy. The state auditor general report informed news outlets that COVID deaths in these long-term care homes were undercounted by 30 percent.[50]

I also believe there was an undisclosed desire within the Republican party to elect a Republican candidate who would align with vaccine mandates. The government's desire to get everyone vaccinated was so pressing that the political leaders were looking for pro-COVID vaccine candidates.

I later discovered that the primary candidates in Michigan's 11th and 8th districts, two of the most contested seats in the state of Michigan, refused to sign the "Michigan for Vaccine Choice" document, declaring how they would vote on this important issue.

During a live online 11th district Republican candidate debate, seen by thousands of viewers, someone hacked the system with homosexual porn. This just shows the depraved minds of some of those connected with the national political discourse.

I stand firm on medical freedom, and any medical treatment should be an individual's choice, not that of the corporation or the government. So many qualified

---

49 "https://www.foxnews.com/politics/whitmer-admin-undercounted-michigan-nursing-home-coviddeaths

50 https://www.foxnews.com/politics/whitmer-admin-undercounted-michigan-nursing-home-covid-deaths

employees in multiple institutions lost their jobs for refusing to compromise their bodies with an experimental vaccine.

Corruption has always run deep in the political world, but what we witnessed in the 2020 election was a gross display of slander, censorship, and media commentary that has left our nation divided. Our country needs Jesus! Our homes need Jesus! We need to come to repentance in a big way. Our nation will not change until people's hearts change. The only hope for our nation and our children is to allow God to work in each of our hearts individually.

Jesus reminds us in John 18:36-37 that His kingdom is not of this world. As much as I think it is important to be a light in this desperate and dying world, we also need to align with heaven and continue to look up because our redemption draws near. John 18:36-37 says:

> Jesus said, "My kingdom is not of this world. If it were, my servants would fight to prevent my arrest by the Jewish leaders. But now my kingdom is from another place."

> "You are a king, then!" said Pilate.

> Jesus answered, "You say that I am a king. In fact, the reason I was born and came into the world is to testify to the truth. Everyone on the side of truth listens to me." (NIV)

Chapter 22
Man Becoming as God

Known thinkers are encouraging mankind to upgrade their DNA, that human 2.0 is the next step in our evolutionary development. One of these premier thinkers is Dr. Yuval Noah Harari, who seems to have a radical distaste for the Abrahamic religions. He says they are myths, and does not give any historical credit to the profound history of the Bible and other religious texts. The men in the Bible existed, however, as there is significant evidence of their stories and lives. Maybe he was too connected to these stories since he grew up in Israel, so now he's looking for alternative realities. When man can't fit his own ideas and morality into the wisdom of the past, he searches for new ideas that redefine family structure, gender, and even democracy.

His book, *Sapiens,* which is well-received by secular thinkers like Bill Gates and Barak Obama, as well as many intellectual groups, is an evolutionary view of the history of mankind. His book brings new understanding of where humans have taken major leaps in their development throughout the evolutionary process and where mankind's future is leading.

His book ties in closely to an atheistic worldview that sees human advancement as a mere accident. Humankind becoming a dominating class of chimpanzees had to find common bonds and myths to believe in order to better relate as a society. The final step in the evolutionary cycle is the scientific revolution that no longer holds tightly to historical religions of the past but merges concepts of God and science to create new religions that feature mere men becoming gods.

Dr. Harari acknowledges there are possible dangers in this new transition. For example, certain classes of people could be recognized as more evolved due to their technological upgrades. There would likely be a large class of humans who are no longer needed in the workforce because technology has taken their place. This dystopian future brings me to the movie Hunger Games where an elite political class controlled the masses. This would also be the fulfillment of the George Orwell's dystopian society, a group of super-evolved humans controlling the masses of undervalued humans.

From a biblical worldview, this evolution of man becoming God is the full expression of eating the apple from the tree of knowledge referred to in Genesis 3. We become so wise in our own eyes that we believe we are gods. With the merging of technology and humans, we can have access to unlimited information from Google and other computer sources: Mankind 2.0.

We must recall in Genesis 3:1-5 that the serpent tricked Eve into choosing her own logical understanding over the wisdom of God, thereby rejecting a complete union with Him:

Now the serpent was more crafty than any of the wild animals the Lord God had made. He said to the woman, "Did God really say, 'You must not eat from any tree in the garden'?"

The woman said to the serpent, "We may eat fruit from the trees in the garden, but God did say, 'You must not eat fruit from the tree that is in the middle of the garden, and you must not touch it, or you will die.'"

"You will not certainly die," the serpent said to the woman. "For God knows that when you eat from it your eyes will be opened, and you will be like God, knowing good and evil." (NIV)

Being like God, knowing good and evil is a deception many still live under today. They seek their own understanding instead of God's truth. While our own understanding and the knowledge of the world are greatly increasing due to technology, they are still limited. Scripture encourages believers to ask, and God will reveal the truth.

We are not limited to our own understanding and logic; we have a divine source of wisdom through our relationship with God. This wisdom is called revelation. Matthew 7:7-8 says "Ask and it will be given to you; seek and you will find; knock and the door will be opened to you. For everyone who asks receives; the one who seeks finds; and to the one who knocks, the door will be opened." (NIV)

James 1:5 adds, "If any of you lacks wisdom, you should ask God, who gives generously to all without finding fault, and it will be given to you." (NIV)

By faith, 1 Corinthians 2:16 says we are also given the mind of Christ through our spiritual conversion: "For who hath known the mind of the Lord, that he may instruct him? But we have the mind of Christ." (KJV)

The mind of Christ naturally opposes the wisdom of the world because it speaks from the revelation of the Spirit. 1 Corinthians 2:14-16 says:

> But the natural man receiveth not the things of the Spirit of God: for they are foolishness unto him: neither can he know them, because they are spiritually discerned. But he that is spiritual judgeth all things, yet he himself is judged of no man. For who hath known the mind of the Lord, that he may instruct him? but we have the mind of Christ. (KJV)

Jesus illustrated this point by speaking in parables. He understood that those thinking with their natural intellect would not discern the deeper spiritual truths the parables revealed. Matthew 13:10-17 says:

The Purpose of Parables

> And the disciples came and said to Him, "Why do You speak to them in parables?"

> He answered and said to them, "Because it has been given to you to know the mysteries of the kingdom of heaven, but to them it has not been given. For whoever has, to him more will be given, and he will have abundance; but whoever does not have, even what he has will be taken away from him. Therefore

I speak to them in parables, because seeing they do not see, and hearing they do not hear, nor do they understand. And in them the prophecy of Isaiah is fulfilled, which says:

'Hearing you will hear and shall not understand, And seeing you will see and not perceive; For the hearts of this people have grown dull *Their ears are hard of hearing,* And their eyes they have closed, Lest they should see with *their* eyes and hear with *their* ears, Lest they should understand with *their* hearts and turn, So that I should heal them.'

But blessed *are* your eyes for they see, and your ears for they hear; for assuredly, I say to you that many prophets and righteous *men* desired to see what you see, and did not see *it,* and to hear what you hear, and did not hear *it.*" (NKJV)

The upgrade of Mankind 2.0 will not heighten our ability to spiritually discern truth. Instead mankind will drift further away from the morality and wisdom of God, and people's minds will become more depraved. Nebuchadnezzar wanted to be exalted and worshipped as God, but a curse came upon him that caused his rational mind to leave him grazing the mountains of Israel as a wild animal for seven years until he recognized that he was not God.

The New Testament also reveals a confusion that comes upon a nation when they do not recognize God as creator; therefore, God leads them to lust after unnatural attractions. Romans 1:24-30 says:

"Therefore, God gave them over in the sinful desires of their hearts to sexual impurity for the degrading of their bodies with one another. They exchanged the truth about God for a lie and worshiped and served created things rather than the Creator—who is forever praised. Amen. Because of this, God gave them over to shameful lusts. Even their women exchanged natural sexual relations for unnatural ones. In the same way the men also abandoned natural relations with women and were inflamed with lust for one another. Men committed shameful acts with other men and received in themselves the due penalty for their error. Furthermore, just as they did not think it worthwhile to retain the knowledge of God, so God gave them over to a depraved mind, so that they do what ought not to be done. They have become filled with every kind of wickedness, evil, greed and depravity. They are full of envy, murder, strife, deceit, and malice. They are gossips, slanderers, God-haters, insolent, arrogant and boastful; they invent ways of doing evil; they disobey their parents;" (NIV)

This verse rings truer today than ever before, as much of mankind has turned its back on God. Failing to exalt God as creator has given many over to a depraved mind that solely recognizes scientific facts when it promotes the political agenda of the evolutionists. Jesus asked the disciples in Luke 18:8, "I tell you, he will see that they get justice, and quickly. However, when the Son of Man comes, will he find faith on the earth?" (NIV)

Scripture reveals that even the elect would be deceived if it were possible. The level of deception is increasing, and believers need to be tuned to the progress of the Anti-Christ's system and the intellect and vain philosophies that are taking people captive. Mankind has arrived at a pivotal hour where people believe they can become gods. Science is also attempting to bring a message of eternal salvation through technology. Soon mankind will be able to upload their brains to the cloud and continue living in an alternate form. These technocrats give no recognition to the eternal soul. Rather they see the mind as the top of the hierarchy of the human body.

Mankind is headed for a big wake-up call! God is rich in His mercy, but He will not be mocked. A man reaps what he sows, and the nations will be judged according to their iniquities.

Chapter 23
Humanity is Hackable

Harari has also mentioned many times that through-out history many governments and tyrants want to be able to hack mankind, but the technology was not available. We have reached the hour where humans are "hackable." Harari says, "In the past, many tyrants and governments wanted to [hack millions of people], but nobody understood biology well enough,"… "And nobody had enough computing power and data to hack millions of people. Neither the Gestapo nor the KGB could do it. But soon, at least some corporations and governments will be able to systematically hack all the people." He goes on to say that "We humans should get used to the idea that we are no longer mysterious souls. We are now hackable animals."[51]

The World Economic Forum (WEF) says the purpose of merging technology with the human body is to bring the ability to monitor human activity and human health. Putting microchips under our skin, for example, could

51 https://www.weforum.org/agenda/2020/01/yuval-hararis-warning-da-vos-speech-future-predications/ and https://www.survivethenews.com/yu-val-noah-harari-humans-are-now-hackable-animals-thanks-to-vaccines/

track the outbreak of a virus. This, of course, would also eliminate personal privacy. Harari sees the coronavirus pandemic as the moment "a new regime of surveillance took over, especially surveillance under the skin."

He further questions to whom all this data belongs: us, a corporation, the government, or a human collective? He is clearly thinking from a communal, socialist point of view. Harari further explains, "The whole idea that humans have, you know…have this soul, spirit, and they have free will and nobody knows what's happening inside me, so whatever I choose, whether in the election or whether in the supermarket, this is my free will, that's over! Free will, that's over!"[52]

Claus Schwab, founder of the WEF relates fully with Dr. Harari's understanding. He says, "The most important development of the 21st century is this ability to hack human beings to go under the skin, collect biometric data, analyze it, and understand people better than they understand themselves. This, I believe, is maybe the most important event of the 21st century. One of the features of this 4th industrial revolution is that it doesn't change what we are doing, but it changes us…if you take your genetic editing, just as an example, it's you who are changed, and, of course, this has a big impact on your identity."[53]

According to the WEF website, "The Fourth the Industrial Revolution, finally, will change not only what we do but

---

52 https://www.youtube.com/watch?v=ltJTRnNLYqY Hebrew University's Prof. Yuval Noah Harari on The Era of the Coronavirus: Living in a New Reality

53 "The Fourth Industrial Revolution: What it Means and How to Respond," a World Economic Forum article by Klaus Schwab, January 14, 2016. https://www.weforum.org/agenda/2016/01/the-fourth-industrial-revolution-what-it-means-and-how-to-respond/

also who we are. It will affect our identity and all the issues associated with it: our sense of privacy, our notions of ownership, our consumption patterns, the time we devote to work and leisure, and how we develop our careers, cultivate our skills, meet people, and nurture relationships. It is already changing our health and leading to a "quantified" self, and sooner than we think it may lead to human augmentation. Now a Fourth Industrial Revolution is building on the Third, the digital revolution that has been occurring since the middle of the last century. It is characterized by a fusion of technologies that is blurring the lines between the physical, digital, and biological spheres."[54]

The WEF and those associated with these ideals are ushering in the darkest hour in human history: an era of mass surveillance, loss of personal autonomy, loss of private property, shifts in identity that could lead to a race of a superhuman elite class controlling a population of human slaves. This conversation may not be of great concern if there wasn't so much money and power behind the WEF's ideas and organization. The WEF is partnered with many of the world's political and economic leaders and top corporations. Black Rock Inc. has more than $10 trillion in assets alone. Bible prophecy watchers have speculated about this moment for hundreds of years, and we see a formulation of the beast system referenced in the book of Revelation coming into fruition.

The Mark of the Beast technology will likely alter the DNA of all who take the mark under their skin. It will be linked to a digital currency, a universal religion, and a universal health and global government platform. Revelation 13:8 & 15-17 says:

---

54 Ibid.

And all that dwell upon the earth shall worship him, whose names are not written in the book of life of the Lamb slain from the foundation of the world.... And he had power to give life unto the image of the beast, that the image of the beast should both speak, and cause that as many as would not worship the image of the beast should be killed. And he causeth all, both small and great, rich and poor, free and bond, to receive a mark in their right hand, or in their foreheads: And that no man might buy or sell, save he that had the mark, or the name of the beast, or the number of his name. (KJV)

The moment has arrived for the church to awaken to the hour of the coming of our Lord Jesus Christ!

Chapter 24
A Wrecking Ball Coming to Hollywood

If you are a parent in 2022, you have likely seen some of the entertainment coming out of Hollywood, the quality of which continues to become more vile, murderous, and perverse year after year. The hearts behind the film creators are revealed in the content they create.

The continued pervasive attack on youth via films and entertainment has reached its fullness, and the courtroom in heaven has reached a verdict. A heavenly judgment will be revealed against Hollywood and this corrupt industry. Lawsuits against the blatant directed attack and manipulation of young minds will be released against the production companies.

These lawsuits will bring Hollywood under the moral accountability that existed in its early years. We can look at the destruction of Nineveh and recognize that God does not allow a culture to remain on a pathway of blatant sin and immorality. According to Exodus 34:5-7, the Lord is rich in mercy and slow to anger, but the guilty will be punished:

> Then the Lord came down in the cloud and stood there with him and proclaimed his name, the Lord. And he passed in front of Moses, proclaiming, "The Lord, the Lord, the compassionate and gracious God, slow to anger, abounding in love and faithfulness, maintaining love to thousands, and forgiving wickedness, rebellion and sin. Yet he does not leave the guilty unpunished; he punishes the children and their children for the sin of the parents to the third and fourth generation." (NIV)

In the early years of the Motion Picture Association (MPA), Congress considered creating a national censorship board due to citizens' complaints about illicit content in films. A U.S. Supreme Court ruling in 1915 decided that films did not qualify for First Amendment protection, so the MPA created the Hays Code in 1930 to appease national tensions and limit obscene film content. The code placed several restrictions on films produced, distributed, or exhibited by the Motion Picture Producers and Distributors of America (MPPDA), today known as the MPA).

Following are the General Principles of the Hays Code:

1. No picture shall be produced which will lower the moral standards of those who see it. Hence the sympathy of the audience should never be thrown to the side of crime, wrongdoing, evil, or sin.
2. Correct standards of life, subject only to the requirements of drama and entertainment, shall be presented.

3. Law, natural or human, shall not be ridiculed, nor shall sympathy be created for its violation.

Particular Applications

I—Crimes Against the Law
These shall never be presented in such a way as to throw sympathy with the crime as against law and justice or to inspire others with a desire for imitation.

1. *Murder*
   a. The technique of murder must be presented in a way that will not inspire imitation.
   b. Brutal killings are not to be presented in detail.
   c. Revenge in modern times shall not be justified.
2. *Methods of Crime* should not be explicitly presented.
   a. Theft; robbery; safe-cracking; and dynamiting of trains, mines, buildings, etc., should not be detailed in method.
   b. Arson must be subject to the same safeguards.
   c. The use of firearms should be restricted to essentials.
   d. Methods of smuggling should not be presented.
3. *Illegal drug traffic* must never be presented.
4. *The use of liquor* in American life, when not required by the plot or for proper characterization will not be shown.

II—Sex
The sanctity of the institution of marriage and the home shall be upheld. Pictures shall not infer that low forms of sex relationship are the accepted or common thing.

1. *Adultery*, sometimes necessary plot material, must not be explicitly treated, or justified, or presented attractively.
2. *Scenes of Passion*
   a. They should not be introduced when not essential to the plot.
   b. Excessive and lustful kissing, lustful embraces, suggestive postures and gestures, are not to be shown.
   c. In general passion should so be treated that these scenes do not stimulate the lower and baser element.
3. *Seduction or Rape*
   a. They should never be more than suggested, and only when essential for the plot, and even then never shown by explicit method.
   b. They are never the proper subject for comedy.
4. Sex perversion or any inference to it is forbidden.
5. *White-slavery* shall not be treated.
6. *Miscegenation* (sex relationships between the white and black races) is forbidden.
7. *Sex hygiene* and venereal diseases are not subjects for motion pictures.
8. Scenes of *actual childbirth,* in fact or in silhouette, are never to be presented.
9. *Children's sex organs* are never to be exposed.

III—Vulgarity

The treatment of low, disgusting, unpleasant, though not necessarily evil, subjects should be subject always to the dictates of good taste and a regard for the sensibilities of the audience.

IV—Obscenity

Obscenity in word, gesture, reference, song, joke, or by suggestion (even when likely to be understood only by part of the audience) is forbidden.

V—Profanity

Pointed profanity (this includes the words, God, Lord, Jesus, Christ—unless used reverently—Hell, S.O.B. damn, Gawd), or every other profane or vulgar expression, however used, is forbidden.

VI—Costume

1. *Complete nudity* is never permitted. This includes nudity in fact or in silhouette, or any lecherous or licentious notice thereof by other characters in the picture.
2. *Undressing scenes* should be avoided, and never used save where essential to the plot.
3. *Indecent or undue exposure* is forbidden.
4. *Dancing costumes* intended to permit undue exposure or indecent movements in the dance are forbidden.

VII—Dances

1. Dances suggesting or representing sexual actions or indecent passion are forbidden.
2. Dances which emphasize indecent movements are to be regarded as obscene.

VIII—Religion

1. No film or episode may throw ridicule on any religious faith.
2. *Ministers of religion* in their character as ministers of religion should not be used as comic characters or as villains.
3. *Ceremonies* of any definite religion should be carefully and respectfully handled.

IX—Locations

The treatment of bedrooms must be governed by good taste and delicacy.

X—National Feelings

1. *The use of the Flag* shall be consistently respectful.
2. *The history,* institutions, prominent people, and citizenry of other nations shall be represented fairly.

XI—Titles

Salacious, indecent, or obscene titles shall not be used.

XII—Repellent Subjects

The following subjects must be treated within the careful limits of good taste:

1. *Actual hangings* or electrocutions as legal punishments for crime.
2. *Third Degree* methods.
3. *Brutality* and possible gruesomeness.
4. *Branding* of people or animals.
5. *Apparent cruelty* to children or animals.
6. *The sale of women* or a woman selling her virtue.
7. *Surgical operations.*[55]

Today, the MPA has broken every part of this moral code. They have worked to bring humanity into moral deprivation and confusion. The arts have a huge influence on culture. As founder of the International Fine Art fund, 501C3 for the promotion of sacred works, I understand firsthand how art can communicate a profound message. The contemporary art communities have deeply neglected the curation of biblical works and dialogue.

In my journey to better understand how devotional works were being presented around the globe, I traveled to many national and international art fairs and museums. I was far pressed to view any major artistic show or platform that showed Jesus Christ in a positive light. During my visit to Art Basel Miami, I saw a gallery presenting a Bible carved in the shape of a gun by artist Robert The.

---

55 "The Motion Picture Production Code of 1930," as quoted in Leonard J. Jeff and Jerold Simmons, eds., *The Dame in the Kimono: Hollywood, Censorship, and the Production Code from the 1920s to the 1960s* (New York: Grove Wiedenfeld, 1990), 283–286.

I felt God calling me to be a light in the deeply cyn-
ical world of contemporary art. I believe in our First
Amendment right to create and speak, but I believe
such blatant attacks on others and their beliefs should
be handled delicately and not be allowed in government and educational institutions.

Art such as motions pictures, which can permeate all
levels of society, especially the youth, should have congressional censorship. Allowing the MPA to censor their own
works has failed. They have gone after sales and thought
nothing of protecting the viewers from harmful content.
Ted Bundy, an infamous serial killer in the 1970s, said that
the media and pornography had a great influence on him
and other prisoners.

According to Bundy, "Those of us who have been so
much influenced by violence in the media, in particular
pornographic violence, are not some kind of inherent
monsters. We are your sons, and we are your husbands.
And we grew up in regular families. And pornography
can reach out and snatch a kid out of any house today.
It snatched me out of my home 20, 30 years ago.... I've
lived in prison for a long time now, and I've met a lot of
men who were motivated to commit violence just like me.
And without exception, every one of them...was deeply involved in pornography."

Most pornography is delivered in the form of film.
Graphic violence is now commonplace in our sitcoms and
movies, and it leads many to think violence is a normal
and acceptable way to solve problems.

Some of our mass guns shootings are likely influenced by films and television as well. We cannot deny
that we live in a violent society because of the violence

being promoted through media arts and culture.

Recently, vice presidents of the Walt Disney company declared their intent to create content to promote the transgender and homosexual agendas to our nation's youth. This is an explicit attempt to influence young minds to adopt and accept an alternative lifestyle. Parents were outraged by this targeted content.

Many young people in America are experiencing identity confusion, and the deliberate attempt to lead more into confusion is very apparent. I have tried to limit movie content within my own family, but it's very difficult for parents in this age of technology. We need to create laws to ensure that mass media content is created with a conscience to protect innocent minds.

Chapter 25
Mystery Babylon

The great city in Revelation 17 and 18 has been grabbing my attention lately. I inquired of God about the coming destruction of the mystery city. If judgment were to come in my lifetime, as I expect based on the fulfillment of biblical prophecy and the reestablishment of the state of Israel, which city best fits the description of Mystery Babylon? Some scholars assume it was Rome because the city is said to sit on seven hills, but it lacks the commerce and does not sit on many waters as described in Revelation 17:1-2:

> One of the seven angels who had the seven bowls came and said to me, "Come, I will show you the punishment of the great prostitute, who sits by many waters. With her the kings of the earth committed adultery, and the inhabitants of the earth were intoxicated with the wine of her adulteries." (NIV)

Babylon was a city of great wealth, trade, idol worship, and people opposed to the will of God just like our modern cities of luxury are today.

Biblically, the word "waters" in the Revelation 17 scripture can mean people and languages. New York city is known for its diverse population, filled with people and languages. The first thing refugees would see upon entering Ellis Island by boat is the great Statue of Liberty.

The inspiration behind the statue was the goddess Ishtar, the goddess of liberty, known as the mother of harlots. It was a gift from the French government. They were initially going to give it to Egypt, but preparation for the statue showed to be too expensive, according to the following article excerpt:

> The first sketch of New York's Statue of Liberty by architect Frédéric Auguste Bartholdi was first intended to represent an "Egyptian peasant in Muslim garments." In his early designs, Bartholdi called the sculpture "Egypt Carrying the Light to Asia." However, Egyptian officials rejected the statue as too expensive, leading the architect to take his plans to America. He had to drop her Islamic robe and transform her into a Roman Goddess, renaming her "Liberty Enlightening the World."[56]

---

56 "New York's Statue of Liberty was meant to be a Muslim woman guarding the Suez Canal" on the Enterprise State of the Nation website, May 17, 2018. https://enterprise.press/stories/2018/05/07/new-yorks-statue-of-liberty-was-meant-to-be-a-muslim-woman-guarding-the-suez-canal/

Architect Frédéric Auguste Bartholdi was a 33rd-degree Mason, and the statue holds the Masonic, torch of enlightenment, presented by the French Grand Temple Masons. In Masonic lore, Lucifer is honored at the light-bearer.

Painting of Lucifer 1797

Statue of Liberty 1875

The seven-star crown represents the crown of Apollo, the Greek sun god. The statue also has an uncanny resemblance to a sixteenth-century painting of Lucifer by Sir Thomas Lawrence (1797), whom Illuminists worship as the light bearer.

The Revelation 17 scripture I quoted previously continues with, "With her all the Kings of the Earth committed adultery." New York City's adulteries and luxuries have been traded with many nations. We as a nation have counted profit as God. If it makes money, we accept it as profitable. Internet pornography in the United States alone is a $3 billion industry.

Worldwide pornography revenue in 2006 was $97.06 billion. Of that, approximately $13 billion was in the United States.[57]

The pornography industry generates $12 billion dollars in annual revenue - larger than the combined annual revenues of ABC, NBC, and CBS. Of that, the Internet pornography industry generates $2.5 billion dollars in annual revenue.[58]

---

57 *Internet Filter Review*, 2006.

58 Pornography Statistics. Family Safe Media. January 10, 2006. http://www.familysafemedia.com/pornography_statistics.html

Revelation 18:22 tells us that mystery Babylon is also a city of music, arts, and trade, much like New York City:

And the voice of harpers, and musicians, and of pipers, and trumpeters, shall be heard no more at all in thee; and no craftsman, of whatsoever craft he be, shall be found any more in thee; and the sound of a millstone shall be heard no more at all in thee; (KJV)

Revelation 17:3-5 continues with:

"There I saw a woman sitting on a scarlet beast that was covered with blasphemous names and had seven heads and ten horns. The woman was dressed in purple and scarlet, and was glittering with gold, precious stones and pearls. She held a golden cup in her hand, filled with abominable things and the filth of her adulteries. The name written on her forehead was a mystery:

Babylon the great
the mother of prostitutes
and of the abominations of the earth." (NIV)

The beast represents a world empire, a reestablishment of a league of ten nations. It's made up of seven regions and ten kings with the woman sitting in authority over the nations. The reestablishment of the Roman empire is the best explanation for this verse. Rome existed as a world empire for nearly two millennia before it was destroyed. The modern alliances of the EU and the establishment of the United Nations could be the representation of a modern Roman empire.

In addition, the United Nations, representing the nations of the world, have historically been located in New York City. The World Trade Center built in 1964 would further mark New York City as the primary place of global trade and international relations prior to its destruction on 9/11/01. So, America sits enthroned as a world power over the nations and the headquarters are in New York City.

Revelation 17:6 could allude to a future persecution of Christians in the City of New York: "I saw that the woman was drunk with the blood of God's holy people, the blood of those who bore testimony to Jesus." (NIV) It could also relate to mass abortions committed in New York City. On January 22, 1999, Governor Cuomo passed the state's historic Reproductive Health Act, which legalized abortion over twenty-four weeks. The government celebrated this new law by illuminating the One World Trade Center in pink. The expansion of this law legalized abortion up to birth if both doctor and patient do not deem the baby viable.

Scripture confirms that God's destiny over His people and His plans for them were written in the womb. Read the message of Isaiah 1:5: "Before I formed thee in the belly I knew thee; and before thou camest forth out of the womb I sanctified thee, and I ordained thee a prophet unto the nations." (KJV)

King Herod tried to kill Jesus at His birth because he knew that Jesus had a special destiny. How many saints have been murdered in womb before they ever had a chance to complete the destiny God had ordained for them?

Chapter 26
There Will Be No Delay!

When Ezekiel pronounced the coming judgment to the nation of Israel in Ezekiel 12:21-28, the people became arrogant because they didn't see a manifestation of these judgments. God rebuked the people, however, and confirmed that these things would surely come to pass with haste:

> The word of the Lord came to me: "Son of man, what is this proverb you have in the land of Israel: 'The days go by and every vision comes to nothing'? Say to them, 'This is what the Sovereign Lord says: I am going to put an end to this proverb, and they will no longer quote it in Israel.' Say to them, 'The days are near when every vision will be fulfilled. For there will be no more false visions or flattering divinations among the people of Israel. But I the Lord will speak what I will, and it shall be fulfilled without delay. For in your days, you rebellious people, I will fulfill whatever I say, declares the Sovereign Lord.'"

The word of the Lord came to me: "Son of man,
the Israelites are saying, 'The vision he sees is for
many years from now, and he prophesies about the
distant future.'

"Therefore say to them, 'This is what the Sovereign Lord says: None of my words will be delayed
any longer; whatever I say will be fulfilled, declares
the Sovereign Lord.'" (NIV)

We are in a similar time when believers have grown
complacent discussing the second coming of Jesus and aspects of Bible prophecy. I sense the Holy Spirit is urging
the church that the time is near, so we cannot afford to be
complacent with our faith.

Revelation 10:5-7 echoes this same haste:

Then the angel I had seen standing on the sea and
on the land raised his right hand to heaven. And he
swore by him who lives for ever and ever, who created the heavens and all that is in them, the earth and
all that is in it, and the sea and all that is in it, and
said, "There will be no more delay! But in the days
when the seventh angel is about to sound his trumpet, the mystery of God will be accomplished, just as
he announced to his servants the prophets." (NIV)

In John 9:4, Jesus emphasized the importance of sharing the gospel while it was accessible. There are times
coming when it will be more difficult to share due to increased persecution. Jesus puts it this way: "As long as it is

day, we must do the works of him who sent me. Night is coming when no one can work." (NIV)

There will be no more delay. There is an urgency to work while it is still daytime. There is an acceleration in the Spirit for those who are coming near to God.

Chapter 27
The Remnant Saved by Grace

The message throughout biblical history reveals that God always spares a remnant of His people. A remnant is a selection of people who have been reserved for the purposes of heaven. These are the people who mourn and lament over the sins of their nation and have received God's eternal forgiveness.

The word *remnant* is first mentioned in Genesis 45:7: "Joseph declared to his brothers, 'But God sent me ahead of you to preserve for you a remnant on earth and to save your lives by a great deliverance.'" (NIV) Jacob's son, Joseph, was sold into slavery and later held the highest position in Pharaoh's household so that God could preserve the Israelites during a time of famine.

The prophet Ezekiel also spoke about a remnant of God's people. He brought many warnings of a coming judgment, and the theme of God sparing a portion of the people is replete throughout Ezekiel's oracles. Ezekiel 3:16-18 contains the message of God calling Ezekiel to be a watchman, one who would sound the alarm of the coming judgment and encourage the nation of Israel to repent for their sins and find God's mercy.

Ezekiel's Task as Watchman

At the end of seven days the word of the Lord came to me: "Son of man, I have made you a watchman for the people of Israel; so hear the word I speak and give them warning from me. When I say to a wicked person, 'You will surely die,' and you do not warn them or speak out to dissuade them from their evil ways in order to save their life, that wicked person will die for their sin, and I will hold you accountable for their blood. But if you do warn the wicked person and they do not turn from their wickedness or from their evil ways, they will die for their sin; but you will have saved yourself. (NIV)

Ezekiel lived out his calling virtuously. He warned the nation many times, and scripture reveals that a remnant received his message and repented from their ways.

In Ezekiel 5:1-4, Ezekiel is asked to shave his hair, representing the people and the judgments that will come upon them. Most of the hair is either being scattered by the wind, as the people will be scattered from their land, while other hairs are burned in the fire, representing death. A remaining few will be tucked away in the folds of his garment, representing the remnant that will be preserved.

God's Razor of Judgment

Now, son of man, take a sharp sword and use it as a barber's razor to shave your head and your beard. Then take a set of scales and divide up the hair. When the days of your siege come to an end, burn a third of the hair inside the city. Take a third and strike it with the sword all around the city. And scatter a third to the wind. For I will pursue them with drawn sword. But take a few hairs and tuck them away in the folds of your garment. Again, take a few of these and throw them into the fire and burn them up. A fire will spread from there to all Israel. (NIV)

Ezekiel 9:4 & 6 also clearly reveals a remnant spared by God's grace. God called seven men to execute judgment upon Israel. Six had a weapon in their hand, and the other was a man clothed in linen with a writing kit at his side. The man of with the writing kit on his side would mark the remnant that would be spared from judgment.

Then the Lord called to the man clothed in linen who had the writing kit at his side and said to him, "Go throughout the city of Jerusalem and put a mark on the foreheads of those who grieve and lament over all the detestable things that are done in it."

"Slaughter the old men, the young men and women, the mothers and children, but do not touch anyone who has the mark. Begin at my sanctuary."

So they began with the old men who were in front of the temple. (NIV)

Roman's 11 shares the mercy God had on a remnant of Israel. God had mercy on this remnant chosen by grace. The 7,000 Israelites had continued loyalty to God and did not bow their knee to Baal.

Don't you know what Scripture says in the passage about Elijah—how he appealed to God against Israel: "Lord, they have killed your prophets and torn down your altars; I am the only one left, and they are trying to kill me"? And what was God's answer to him? "I have reserved for myself seven thousand who have not bowed the knee to Baal." So too, at the present time there is a remnant chosen by grace. And if by grace, then it cannot be based on works; if it were, grace would no longer be grace. (NIV)

To this day, there is a remnant chosen by grace, those that have a continued devotion to God. God is provoking hearts to return to him and be included in this great number of saints.

Chapter 28
A Church United In Spirit And Truth

God is calling for His church to rise in a spirit of unity and revelation that will oppose the coming world order. His Spirit is awakening and linking hearts and minds and unveiling eyes to remove denominational walls, separate the wheat from the chaff, and lead His people into His presence.

The Spirit of God was poured out on the first century church when it came together in one accord in the upper room. Acts 2:1-3 says:

> And when the day of Pentecost was fully come, they were all with one accord in one place. And suddenly there came a sound from heaven as of a rushing mighty wind, and it filled all the house where they were sitting. And there appeared unto them cloven tongues like as of fire, and it sat upon each of them. (KJV)

There is a true blessing the Holy Spirit brings when brothers and sitters dwell together in unity. This requires walking in a love that we may not fully know at this hour. The Spirit of God will settle all doctrinal issues with the refiner's fire. We need an outpouring of His Spirit.

Persecution may preclude the separation of the wheat from the chaff, and only those truly committed to Christ will be left standing. Matthew 3:12 says, "His winnowing fork is in his hand, and he will clear his threshing floor, gathering his wheat into the barn and burning up the chaff with unquenchable fire." (NIV)

The wheat are those who are following the voice of the Lord, and the chaff are following the ways of world and the leading of man. We cannot depend on following the voice of men. We need to seek truth and discern the voice of God for ourselves. John 10:27 says, "My sheep listen to my voice; I know them, and they follow me." (NIV)

Approximately ten years ago, I had a dream that still plays in my thoughts. I saw Christian people fighting amongst each other, even to the point of death, at some point in the past. The disagreements were so evident they ended in brutal acts of violence. The scene transitioned to a large theatre dance performance. The same people who were brutally beating each other needed to dance together in this great performance. I was one of the dancers. They had to mend the past and move on to perform kindly with each other.

I woke from the dream a little perplexed, but I asked God for understanding. I understood that the dancers represented sects of Christianity that had been at war with each other. They would come together for an end-time performance ushering in the return of Christ. They will be God's chosen people, those who are seeking God's truth, who will be called out from the masses to watch for the return of Christ.

True followers of Christ are led by His Spirit to unite as one body with many parts as 1 Corinthians 12:12-25 says:

Unity and Diversity in the Body

Just as a body, though one, has many parts, but all its many parts form one body, so it is with Christ. For we were all baptized by one Spirit so as to form one body—whether Jews or Gentiles, slave or free—and we were all given the one Spirit to drink. Even so the body is not made up of one part but of many.

Now if the foot should say, "Because I am not a hand, I do not belong to the body," it would not for that reason stop being part of the body. And if the ear should say, "Because I am not an eye, I do not belong to the body," it would not for that reason stop being part of the body. If the whole body were an eye, where would the sense of hearing be? If the whole body were an ear, where would the sense of smell be? But in fact God has placed the parts in the body, every one of them, just as he wanted them to be. If they were all one part, where would the body be? As it is, there are many parts, but one body.

The eye cannot say to the hand, "I don't need you!" And the head cannot say to the feet, "I don't need you!" On the contrary, those parts of the body that seem to be weaker are indispensable, and the parts that we think are less honorable we treat with special honor. And the parts that are unpresentable are treated with special modesty, while our presentable parts need no special treatment. But God has put the body together, giving greater honor to the parts that lacked it, so that there should be no division in the body, but that its parts should have equal concern for each other. (NIV)

Jesus is the head of the church as Colossians 1:18 says: "And he is the head of the body, the church; he is the beginning and the firstborn from among the dead, so that in everything he might have the supremacy." (NIV)

I have noticed that many Catholics are coming to know Jesus personally through His Word. This largely due to the recent heretical reforms of Pope Francis, one of the premier cheerleaders for a global government, which have opened the eyes of faithful followers and caused them to depart from the Catholic Church. Pope Francis has aggressively worked to unite world religions. His recent project, the Abrahamic Family House in Abu Dhabi, set to open in 2022, will feature a church, a mosque, and a synagogue in one general area. Many see these initiatives as part of a calculated push toward a one world religion prophesied in the book of Revelation.[59]

Some of the most vocal opponents of the coming world government have been Catholic clergy calling out corruption within the church and revealing globalist

---

59 "Abrahamic Family House in Abu Dhabi to open in 2022," an article on the Vatican News website by Robin Gomes, February 2019. https://www. vaticannews.va/en/vatican-city/news/2021-06/abu-dhabi-abrahamic-family-house-2022-human-fraternity.html

plans. The Reformation of 1517 brought a clear break from the Catholic church to purify the corruption within it. Today many Catholics still identifying as Catholic are seeking truth for themselves and finding greater unity with the body of Christ.

One of the most prominent voices in Catholic leadership is Archbishop Carlo Maria Viganò, who served as the Apostolic Nuncio to the United States from October 19, 2011 to April 12, 2016. He has been a strong voice against the politics of Pope Francis and his plans to bring a universal interfaith religion under the arm of global government.

In fact, he wrote an alarming letter to President Trump, warning him that the COVID-19 pandemic was being used to usher in a world government resulting in permanent loss of personal freedoms. He also launched a website, called the Appeal for the Church and the World, that called for people of goodwill to guard against tyranny. It garnered signatures from 40,000 Catholic prelates, journalists, writers, immunologists, virologists, researchers, attorneys, and others. Then he wrote another open letter that encouraged the President in his fight against the "deep State" followed by a third letter urging Trump to fight against the "Great Reset," an oncoming "health dictatorship."[60]

Never has such prominent international voices revolted against tyranny like I have seen in recent years. The COVID pandemic brought a new level of control over a free citizenship as healthy people were locked in their homes for months, many were put in jail for not adhering

---

60 "Abp. Vigano Pens Open Letter to Trump: Resist 'The Great Reset,'" an article on the Church Militant website by Abp. Carlo Maria Viganò, October 30, 2020. https://www.churchmilitant.com/news/article/open-letter-to-trump-resist-the-great-reset

to new health rules, and hundreds of thousands of qualified workers lost their jobs for not conforming to vaccine mandates that were later shown to be ineffective in stopping the virus. This pandemic gave rise to a stronger arm of government, leaving the population at the mercy of the World Health Organization.

The Archbishop also said that globalist elites are escalating the Ukrainian war for their own gains. Vigano said in his letter that Putin has been cornered by an aggressive NATO, backed by the United States, which is seeking to escalate the conflict for its own gains. "This is the trap for Russia just as much as Ukraine, using both to allow a globalist elite to bring its criminal plot to fruition."[61]

A global deception requires a global awakening, we can't just take the advice of others. We need to seek God for ourselves through the true "High Priest," Jesus Christ. He is the only intermediary between God and man, and we exalt this honor by praying in His name. We will need this unhindered relationship for the times ahead.

Many Christians have gone to YouTube and other social media platforms to share the dreams and visions being released through the Holy Spirit. These platforms are giving access to a global community of believers that are coming together in one Spirit.

I have had the pleasure of connecting with churches and ministers in England and Ireland through social media. These relationships have been encouraging and

---

61 "Viganò, Vatican critic, blames 'deep state' for Ukraine war, citing COVID-19 measures," a *National Catholic Reporter* article by Claire Giangrave, March 18, 2022. https://www.ncronline.org/news/people/vigan-vatican-critic-blames-deep-state-ukraine-war-citing-covid-19-measures

informative. Through technology, the church can link arms all over the globe.

This of course is not accessible where the internet is blocked by government authorities like communist China. Part of the globalist initiative is to limit internet access by running disinformation campaigns, limiting alternative world views that descent from popular opinion, and even labeling the Bible as hate speech.

John 9:4 warns the church to work while it is still daylight. Our freedoms and access to share the gospel in its authentic form are not readily accessible in all nations.

It is important for the body of Christ to come together in the end times because there is no repentance for allegiance to the coming beast system. This global spiritual awakening will ready the church to stand against the plot of the enemy and to put all their hope in Jesus Christ our Lord.

Chapter 29
The People Will Return!

The promise in all this shaking that is coming upon the land is that the people will return to God. America will have a great revival of souls and millions will come to Lord. Many great men and women have prophesied this final great revival. The seed that has been planted in the land will bear a great harvest. Many will leave their New Age teachings and eastern philosophies for the truth of God's redeeming Word.

Evangelist Reinhard Bonnke prophesied in early Feburary of 2013 that America would be saved. He declared this over Africa and saw over 55 million souls come to the Lord. I believe the great shaking that is here has prepared many American souls for the harvest!

Psalm 91:1-2 says "He who dwells in the secret place of the Most High Shall abide under the shadow of the Almighty. I will say of the Lord, "*He is* my refuge and my fortress; My God, in Him I will trust." (NKJV) When reliance on the world's system proves to be faulty, many will seek God in their place of desperation. Matthew 5:4 says,

"Blessed *are* those who mourn, For they shall be comforted." (NKJV)

America's true source of blessing and hope will be restored! The Lord has encouraged me in this word, over and over. The people will return. The people will return! I continue to get this impression on my spirit.

Nahum 1:7 says, "The LORD is good, a stronghold in the day of trouble; he knows those who take refuge in him." (ESV)

Romans 10:13 says, "Everyone who calls on the name of the Lord will be saved." (NIV)

And Joel 2:32 says, "And it shall come to pass that everyone who calls on the name of the Lord shall be saved. For in Mount Zion and in Jerusalem there shall be those who escape, as the Lord has said, and among the survivors shall be those whom the Lord calls." (ESV)

God's judgment is an opportunity for our nation to return to Him. Judgment is a restoration of God's justice in the land. 1 Chronicles 29:11 says: "Yours, Lord, is the greatness and the power and the glory and the majesty and the splendor, for everything in heaven and earth is yours. Yours, Lord, is the kingdom; you are exalted as head over All." (NIV)

www.ingramcontent.com/pod-product-compliance
Lightning Source LLC
LaVergne TN
LVHW051627080426
835511LV00016B/2217